NEW JERSEY
VANGUARD

NEW JERSEY
VANGUARD

FAMOUS FIGURES WHO SHAPED THE NATION

JIM CULLEN

THE
History
PRESS

Published by The History Press
Charleston, SC
www.historypress.com

Front cover, clockwise from top left: Thomas Edison, Jonathan Edwards, Clara Barton, Paul Robeson, Meryl Streep, Walt Whitman.
Back cover, top to bottom: George Washington at the Battle of Trenton, Whitney Houston, Woodrow Wilson and William Jennings Bryan.

First published 2025

Manufactured in the United States

ISBN 9781467156622

Library of Congress Control Number: 2024949769

For Tod Sizer

Heart of New England
Soul of New Jersey

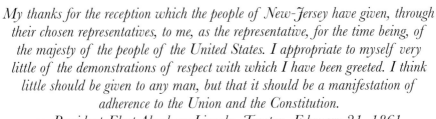

My thanks for the reception which the people of New-Jersey have given, through their chosen representatives, to me, as the representative, for the time being, of the majesty of the people of the United States. I appropriate to myself very little of the demonstrations of respect with which I have been greeted. I think little should be given to any man, but that it should be a manifestation of adherence to the Union and the Constitution.
—President-Elect Abraham Lincoln, Trenton, February 21, 1861

CONTENTS

CONTENTS

ACKNOWLEDGEMENTS

This book began as a project with Peter Mickulas of Rutgers University Press. Though it was not published under his aegis, I am nevertheless grateful to him for the stimulus to get it going.

The fact that it *did* get going is due to Banks Smither and the staff of The History Press. My thanks to all concerned for their goodwill and professionalism, especially Joe Gartrell, who shepherded the project into the production pipeline, and Abigail Fleming, who copyedited the manuscript.

Since 2020, Greenwich Country Day School has been my home. And a fine one it is—my thanks to the students, staff and my wonderful colleagues. Particular thanks to my dear friend Louise Wales, who helped with photos.

Love always to my family—Jay and Natasha (who are expecting their first child), Grayson, Ryland and Nancy—for their company and patience. My final thanks go, as always, to Lyde Sizer.

Jim Cullen
Hastings-on-Hudson, New York
November 2024

INTRODUCTION

MIDDLE STATE

This story, like a great many stories about New Jersey, begins overseas with a place in the middle.

The island of Jersey—officially known as the Bailiwick of Jersey—is located in the English Channel between Great Britain and France (in fact, closer to the latter than the former). Though it is one of the British Isles, Jersey does not belong to the United Kingdom but is rather a self-governing Dependency of the British Crown. Originally part of the French duchy of Normandy, the island has pledged its loyalty to England since the thirteenth century, an identity reflected in language, currency and the fact that cars drive on the left. Jersey was caught between centuries of warfare between England and France and has been occupied a number of times, most recently by the Germans for five years during the Second World War.

During the English Civil Wars of the mid-seventeenth century, Jersey was ruled by George Carteret, who had served as comptroller of the English navy and as an ally of the of the exiled King Charles the II. When Charles ascended to the throne in the Restoration of 1660, his brother (and future King) James, the Duke of York, gave Carteret a tract of land in the American colonies between the Hudson and Delaware Rivers. James dubbed it as the colony of New Jersey (more on this, and the complications surrounding it, in chapter 1). And so it is that a middling place on one side of the world became the namesake of middling place on the other.

This middling status is multilayered. New Jersey began its life as part of an English empire sandwiched between two more powerful ones: France to the north and Spain to the south. Even *within* the English (later British) empire, it occupied a middle zone between relatively homogeneous mercantile New England colonies above and the agrarian, racially segmented South below. New Jersey's middle status goes one step further: it was right smack in the middle of the so-called Middle Colonies, wedged between the much larger New York and Pennsylvania, jostling between the other small middle ones of Delaware and Maryland.

Indeed, New Jersey's significance can seem to rest on its relative insignificance. The state is smaller than forty-five of the fifty in the Union; its population falls somewhere in the middle of the pack. It occupies a mere sliver of Atlantic coastline. And yet while the state is certainly right smack in the middle of that seaboard, one could hardly call it the heartland of a continental nation that stretches three thousand miles to a different coastline, part of a Pacific rim that is now emerging at the focal point on the globe.

But one can turn also such characterizations of New Jersey inside out and say that the state sits at the very heart of the nation and its history. The mixed economy and demographic diversity that have defined the United States have been hallmarks of New Jersey from its very origins. It also sits at the crossroads of the most important structural shifts in American history: from farm to factory, from country to city, from city to suburb. Slavery to freedom, agriculture to industry, manufacturing to services, services to information—it all happened here. New Jersey is literally a crossroads as well, a node of transportation in terms of shipping, rail, interstates and fiber-optic cable. It's not necessarily unique in these regards—but its very typicality, its utter ordinariness, is why it matters. To paraphrase Walt Whitman (the subject of chapter 6), New Jersey is large; it contains multitudes. It is a synecdoche for America.

Like other American places, New Jersey has its native sons and daughters. But it was also a place where a great many Americans found themselves, by accident or choice, at key moments in their lives. It is this alchemy between native and adopted, lifelong and temporary, that gives a place its sense of texture and significance.

And provides the occasion for this book. *New Jersey Vanguard* is a study that spans four hundred years of history to explore how this Middle State became a crucible for a dozen American lives. Sometimes these are origin stories; sometimes New Jersey is the place where life stories ended. In other cases, it was a crossroads, a place where choices were clarified, decisions were made, courses were changed. In the pages that follow, you will encounter people who dedicated their lives to politics, the arts, religion, scholarship and the military, among other pursuits. Each in their way were paragons of excellence, though all were deeply human. As such, their stories illuminate ours.

And so it is that we begin—in the middle.

PROLOGUE

FOUNDING FATHERS SHARE A BED IN MIDDLESEX COUNTY

S o there they are, *John Adams and Benjamin Franklin, one a youthful seventy and the other a fussy forty-one.*[1] *They're at roughly the halfway point in a journey from Philadelphia to Staten Island, part of a delegation sent by the Continental Congress to negotiate with Admiral Lord Richard Howe of the Royal Navy in the hopes of ending the war between England and its American colonies. Two weeks earlier, George Washington's fledgling army escaped seemingly certain destruction in Brooklyn and is for now, at least, alive to fight another day, though it increasingly looks like his ragtag army will be retreating from one end of New Jersey to the other—if they make it that far.*

Lord Howe, who, with his brother General William Howe, has deep ties to the colonies—Franklin used to play chess with their sister Caroline back in London—hopes he can talk his American friends out of making a huge mistake. Adams considers Howe a phony, his overtures nothing more than Machiavellian maneuvers. That's why he was chosen to be one of the negotiators. Edward Rutledge of South Carolina, a man who had been reluctant to support independence (he worried about the preservation of slavery) is another. And Franklin, the obvious choice for a sensitive diplomatic mission, is the third, positioned ideologically and temperamentally between them. Despite their setbacks and the differences between them, the trio is in no mood to compromise.

It is the evening of September 9, 1776. The negotiators pause in their journey to spend the night in Brunswick, where a new college has recently been chartered (Route 18 runs through the site today).

Unfortunately, there's not much lodging to be had in the local taverns. Franklin and Adams agree to share a tiny room, no fireplace, with a single bed and a single open window at an establishment that appears to have been the Indian Queen Inn.[2] *It's chilly, and*

REVOLUTIONARY: Site where John Adams and Benjamin Franklin stayed in 1776. It was torn down to build Route 18 in New Brunswick. *Library of Congress.*

RECONSTRUCTION PROJECT: In the 1970s, the Indian Queen Tavern was moved and rebuilt at East Jersey Old Towne historical park in Piscataway. *Jim Cullen.*

Adams, a self-described invalid, is "afraid of the air in the night" and shuts it. "Oh!" says Franklin. "Don't shut the window. We shall be suffocated." When Adams relates his fears of coming down with an illness from the bad night air, Franklin, ever the scientist, replies by saying that the air in the room is far more likely to be a problem than that outside. "Come!" he tells Adams. "Open the window and come to bed and I will convince you. I believe you are not acquainted with my Theory of Colds."

Adams complies and joins Franklin in bed. He is curious, even at "the risqué of a cold," to hear Franklin's reasoning. Lying there in the dark, side by side, Franklin begins his explanation, which, while apparently of some interest to Adams, literally puts him to sleep. ("I left him and his Philosophy together," he would later write, hearing Franklin trail off just as he does.) They will argue the point again, and in his account of their exchanges Adams muses on Franklin's reasoning but remains unconvinced.

At this point in his life, Adams admires Franklin. He likes to say that had Franklin done nothing more than invent the lightning rod, the world would justly honor this "great and good man." But the next time they team up, this time in Paris to negotiate an alliance with the French government, Adams begins to have his doubts. Mr. "Early to Bed and Early to Rise" sleeps late all the time. (He slept through a lot of the Continental Congress, and though Adams will not be there to catch him, Franklin will sleep through a lot of the Constitutional Convention as well.) He drinks too much; he spends too much. And his behavior with French women is downright embarrassing. Adams feels self-conscious about his French, but as he learns it himself, he begins to realize that Franklin understands a lot less than he lets on. And when Adams—once again the bad cop—annoys the French foreign minister, Franklin writes a letter to Congress telling them that Adams is damaging Franklin's own delicate diplomacy. Adams will never forget or forgive Franklin for that.

Franklin is probably right to dump Adams. Adams probably knows Franklin is right, too. Adams is an intelligent and decent man. But he's too stubborn, too moralistic and too vain to be a successful diplomat. He's honest to a fault—he can't play the game the way Franklin, who laughs right along when the king puts his image on the bottom of his courtesan's chamber pot, does. He tries not to lie, even to himself.

Part of the reason why someone like Franklin is such a trial to Adams is that he understands that Franklin really does have traits Adams himself would be lucky to have. Franklin's cool cheerfulness is a rebuke to Adams's repressed stolidity. But a hunger for recognition, a hunger that's never really sated, will not give Adams rest. His wonderfully acidic expression of resentment in 1790 encapsulates his frustration: "The history of our Revolution will be one continued lie from one end to the other. The essence of the whole will be that Dr. Franklin's electrical rod smote the earth and out sprang General Washington. That Franklin electrified him with his rod and thenceforth these two conducted all the policy, negotiations, legislatures, and war." (It was Adams who

DOUBLE OCCUPANCY: Olde Towne re-creation of the room shared by Adams and Franklin during their diplomatic mission with the British. *Jim Cullen.*

had proposed Washington take command of the Continental army—an excellent idea, notwithstanding the military disaster unfolding in New Jersey, and one he can't help but partially regret.)

Adams had about as successful a career as any person could ever rationally hope. From modest beginnings as a shoemaker's son, he became a self-educated lawyer, political activist and diplomat. He collaborated with Thomas Jefferson on the Declaration of Independence, and his work on the Massachusetts Constitution was a major influence on the federal one. He managed to spend eight years generally keeping his mouth shut as vice president (no small achievement, particularly for him), and went on to become president himself. And he had the good sense and good fortune to marry Abigail, who brought wisdom, humor and joy into his life. He lived to see his son John Quincy become president. We should all be so lucky.

But somehow, you rarely get the impression that John Adams was happy. To be sure, he had legitimate sorrows, among them a son who drank himself to death and a daughter who died of cancer. He had powerful enemies, notably Alexander Hamilton and, for a time, Thomas Jefferson, who, despite hating each other, worked to deny Adams a second term as president. (It's to their credit that Adams and Jefferson were later able to patch things up—though perhaps it's no accident that they did so while remaining five hundred miles apart.) Still, you get the sense that the hardest single thing about John Adams's life is that he had to live with John Adams. Feeling that way is hard enough. But it's even harder when you've got people like Franklin, so seemingly self-assured, by your side.

Adams recorded the scene of his night in Middlesex County with Franklin in the autobiography he began writing after his forced retirement from politics following his failed bid for re-election in 1800. (It was during that year that he returned to Brunswick, this time with Abigail, and appears to have stayed in the same inn had had visited twenty-four years earlier.) Though he had a diary to draw on, the editor of the Adams Papers, L.H. Butterfield, reported in 1961 that Adams wrote this scene "from unaided memory." I see him at his estate, Peacefield, in Quincy, Massachusetts, an old man remembering himself as a younger one, with Franklin, who had been dead for years, alive and likeable. Adams had been upset earlier that September day by what he regarded as the indiscipline and "dissipation" of the American troops he had seen on the road (he was probably prudishly unrealistic). But Adams was "determined that it should not dishearten me." It seems like he's succeeded, and that the memory of that night in New Jersey brings him pleasure and maybe even comfort in the long twilight of his life. Writing it down gives him something to do. Sort of like writing a book. Or reading one.

1

DIRECTOR-GENERAL STUYVESANT CROSSES THE DELAWARE

A DUTCH LEADER LAUNCHES AN ATTACK ON THE WILD WEST FRONTIER OF NEW SWEDEN

The place that became New Jersey, like the other forty-nine United States of America, has had borders that were porous, contested and uncertain. This was true long before Europeans landed on North American shores—the Indigenous Susquehannock and Lenape peoples tussled over territory in what is now known as the Delaware Valley, to cite one example—and even more so once the Spanish, French and English arrived on the Atlantic Seaboard. The colonial claims of each of these empires were loosely clear by about 1650: the Spanish considered much of the interior, along with both coasts of Florida, as their domain; the French colonized eastern Canada and trade routes including the Mississippi River; and the English occupied New England. Ownership over the Eastern Seaboard between modern-day Connecticut and Virginia was a good deal hazier, however. The English claimed all of it; in 1610, the English navigator Samuel Argall explored the bay we now know as Cape May. He named it after Thomas West, the Baron De La Warr, which got bowdlerized into Delaware—future name of a state, river and an English moniker for the Lenape peoples in the area. But the English lacked effective power the region (this was true for a great deal of European claims over vast stretches of the continent). And none of the local Indigenous peoples had the power

GOING DUTCH: Peter Stuyvesant, circa 1660. Director-general of New Netherland, his domain stretched from western Connecticut to southern New Jersey. *Wikimedia Commons.*

and projection of the Iroquois Confederacy that dominated much of northeastern North America.

Into this vacuum came a rising power: the United Provinces of the Dutch Republic. But it was not alone. Yet another European power, this one at the crest of its military might, also edged into the picture: the kingdom of Sweden. For seventeen years, the Swedes held dominion over a territory that straddled the contemporary boundaries of New Jersey and Delaware. They did so until one man led a military expedition to take it back. That man, Peter Stuyvesant, is often considered a founding father of the place we have come to know as New York—for good reason (even if he knew it as New Amsterdam). But Stuyvesant also played a key role in the making of New Jersey, illustrating how volatile its identity was. It's worth a look to see how he gained, maintained, and eventually lost a keystone stretch of mid-Atlantic landscape that became the linchpin of a rising nation.

LIKE THE AMERICAN TERRITORY it would occupy, the Dutch Republic was also a marginal place, a borderland between empires. For centuries, the region was known as the "Low Countries"—a fragmentary set of principalities that has included Belgium, the Netherlands and Luxembourg (hence the term "Benelux"), sandwiched between France and the Holy Roman Empire. The lowness referred to their sea level but also reflected their status as a cat's-paw of larger powers. As the Age of Exploration began, the Low Countries were controlled by the powerful Habsburg emperor Charles V, who bequeathed them to his son Philip II, ruler of the Spanish empire at its zenith. That zenith also corresponded to the outbreak of the Reformation, a religious revolution with significant geopolitical consequences.

One of those consequences was a Dutch bid for independence. This was complicated; some parts of the region, like Belgium, remained largely Catholic, while others—specifically Gelderland, Holland, Zeeland, Utrecht, Friesland, Overijssel and Groningen—formed the core of the Dutch Republic and the Dutch Reformed Church, one in a series of Protestant offshoots that followed in the wake of Martin Luther's theological rebellion. The emergence of that republic was the product of an often vicious eighty-year struggle for independence that only became internationally recognized in 1648, though well before that it was becoming apparent that these new Netherlands were an emerging commercial powerhouse and a significant innovator in the shipping and insurance industries, with Amsterdam as a rising financial center alongside Rotterdam and Antwerp.

By the start of the seventeenth century, the Dutch Republic had become a superpower whose mercantile and naval power projected around the globe. Its crown jewel was the Dutch East India Company, a government-sponsored private corporation founded in 1602 that dominated European trade in Asia for the rest of the century. Like any prosperous enterprise seeking to sustain its growth—and like its European rivals looking for shortcuts to access the China trade—the company looked for new routes and markets. It commissioned the recently cashiered explorer Henry Hudson of the English Muscovy Company to continue his expeditions in the North Atlantic in his obsessive quest to find the fabled Northwest Passage to China. In 1609, Hudson's ship, the *Half Moon*, sailed up the river that now bears his name. He soon realized the river was a dead end as far as China was concerned, but his refusal to give up looking for another passage led his crew leave him and his son behind to perish two years later in the icy Canadian waters of what would be named Hudson Bay.

Meanwhile, a series of rival companies followed in Hudson's wake, seeking to exploit the commercial possibilities in the lower Hudson Valley. The government granted a three-year monopoly to a particular firm, the New Netherland Company, for the fur trade. The ambit of the company's operation was a strip of the river bounded by Nassau (later Albany) in the north and Nut (now Governor's) Island in the south, where the estuary empties into the Atlantic. The company quickly established a lucrative beaver trade with the Munsee peoples of the region. The expiration of its grant in 1617, coupled with geopolitical maneuvering with Spain, led to the Dutch government to give control of the fur trade to the better-capitalized Dutch West India Company. Shares in the company sold quickly, and settlers seeking to work for it began arriving in the early 1620s, clustering around what we now know as New Jersey and Long Island. The Dutch government formally created a colony named New Netherland in 1623.

At least in theory, the Dutch colony of New Netherland had fairly distinct boundaries. Its eastern border was the Connecticut River, which abutted territory that would become the English colony of Hartford. The southern and western border of New Netherland was Delaware Bay, where that river meets the Atlantic. In between was the heart of the colony, a stretch of the Hudson River running about one hundred miles from Manhattan to Nassau. At the time and long after, the Hudson was known as the North River; the Delaware, by contrast, was known as the South River.

Of the two, the North River was far more important in terms of population, trade and strategic value. In the 1620s, a series of settlements sprang up on either side of the South River, most of them populated by ethnically French-speaking (Dutch) Walloons. But the Dutch hold on this territory was tenuous. For about a decade and a half, that didn't particularly matter, because no one was likely—or, perhaps more accurately, had sufficient power—to challenge this set of arrangements. A military installation, Fort Nassau, was built on the eastern (we'll call it the Jersey) shore at the mouth of the river.

The first director the Dutch West India Company—the de facto governor of New Netherland—was Cornelis Jacobszoon May (1624–25). May, along with explorer Cornelis Hendrickson, had navigated the area in 1616 and 1620, returning with a group of religious refugees in 1624 who settled at Manhattan, Fort Orange and Burlington Island, which sits on the Delaware River between what is now New Jersey and Pennsylvania and had once been considered as the seat of Dutch government in the colony. May also ordered the construction of Fort Nassau. Cape May was named in his honor.[3] May was succeeded by Willem Verhulst (1625–26), who was unpopular with the governing council of the colony and was banished.

The next director of the Dutch West India Company, Peter Minuit (1626–31), was among its most consequential. It was he who apparently cut the deal with the Munsee people for the island of Manhattan (some accounts suggest it was Verhulst), where the colony's capital of New Amsterdam took root, protected by a stone boundary on its northern border at what is now Wall Street. Minuit also arranged for the purchase of other crucial real estate, including Staten Island and tracts of land along the Hudson and South Rivers.[4]

But Minuit lost his job. One problem is that while the colony's population was growing and international trade was taking root, the settlement was not turning a profit. Some, among them Minuit, believed that the key to its success involved recruiting wealthy Dutch patrons, or patroons, to establish large plantations and literally and figuratively invest in the company. Patroonships were in fact established in what are now Bergen and Hudson Counties. But Minuit's opponents believed privileging rich settlers would fragment the colony and leave it vulnerable to pirates and renegade traders who would divide and conquer it.[5] This faction succeeded in recalling Minuit, who in 1632 returned to Holland, fuming. He was determined to return and later did—in a most unexpected way, to be discussed later.

GOING SCANDINAVIAN: Peter Minuit (1580–1638). The former director of New Netherland angered former allies upon founding New Sweden on the banks of the Delaware River. *Wikimedia Commons*.

Meanwhile, in 1638, leadership of New Netherland was given to Willem Kieft, who held the job for the next nine years. They were stormy ones. While previous leaders of the colony bought land from local Indians and traded with them, Kieft pushed them to pay taxes for protection and resorted to strong-armed tactics when he didn't get his way. Perhaps the most notorious act of Kieft's directorship occurred in 1643, when a group of Wiechquaeskeck people, harried by their northern neighbors, took refuge in Pavonia, in what is now Jersey City. Rather than protect them, Kieft led a murderous raid. Angry Lenapes counterattacked throughout the region.[6]

Amid this internal upheaval, New Netherlands was also confronted by the challenge of yet another European rival. In the mid-seventeenth century, the kingdom of Sweden under the leadership of King Gustavus Adolphus (1611–32) and his daughter Queen Christiana (1632–54) dominated Scandinavia and parts of modern-day Germany, Poland and Russia. Gustavus Adolphus jealously eyed his rivals' empires in America. He died in battle before he could act on his plan, but his chancellor, Axel Oxenstierna, served as Christiana's regent and plotted a path forward.

That path ran through trade and, more specifically, the Swedes' major trading partner, the Dutch. Oxenstierna came into contact with a Dutch trader named Samuel Blommaert, a director of the West India Company frustrated by missed opportunities in New Netherland. He in turn reached out to Peter Minuit, still smarting from his removal. Minuit, who knew that Dutch settlement near the South River was sparse and vulnerable, put together a military campaign and in March 1638 led a naval expedition under a Swedish flag that landed somewhere near modern-day Wilmington, Delaware, and proclaimed the colony of New Sweden. The Dutch surrendered without a fight. Minuit cut deals with Indigenous tribes, less as a matter of gaining standing with them than flanking Dutch legal maneuvers, especially on the west side of the Delaware, where they had not secured title. Back in New Amsterdam, Kieft issued a manifesto protesting the raid and implied it would be met with force ("we shall maintain our jurisdiction in such as manner, as we shall deem most expedient"). But Minuit ignored it. Leaving behind a garrison, he headed to Europe, where he hoped to recruit Swedish and German settlers for his grand experiment. But in August 1638, Minuit died in a hurricane in the Caribbean, where he had sailed to acquire tobacco that he hoped to

MIXED HERITAGE: Swedish, Dutch and American flags fly outside the Salem County Historical Society building. *Jim Cullen.*

trade back in Europe. So it was that the new colony lost its most energetic booster. Still, over the course of the next decade and a half, New Sweden became a colony of approximately four hundred fur traders and tobacco planters on either side of the Delaware River reaching as far as far north as modern-day Trenton and as far south as contemporary Philadelphia.[7]

New Netherland, meanwhile, limped along in the 1640s. New Amsterdam was its most established settlement, but it was a company town run by the Dutch West India Company, and the settlement's residents were more employees than citizens. Compared with the Jesuits of Quebec or the Puritans of Massachusetts, the Dutch were little more than an ad hoc imperialists struggling to compete in the fur trade. The spine of the colony ran along the Hudson River, where patroons with names like Van Cortland, Schuyler and Rensselaer established vast estates. The place we know as New Jersey was a Dutch outpost on what was still a wild frontier, particularly south of Manhattan.

Dutch imperial fortunes took a turn following Kieft's recall in 1649, when he was replaced by the truly pivotal figure in the history of the colony: Peter Stuyvesant.

Peter Stuyvesant was born about 1610 in the Dutch province of Friesland. He was university educated and went to Amsterdam at age twenty to work for the Dutch West India Company. The company sent him to a variety of sites in Brazil, notably Curaçao, a colony he ran with an iron fist. In 1644, Stuyvesant led an attack on the island of Saint Martin, which the Dutch had lost to the Spanish. His leg was shattered by a cannonball, and he returned to the Netherlands, where he was fitted with the wooden peg for which he would become famous. The following year, he was appointed Kieft's successor in New Netherland and arrived in New Amsterdam in 1647. He would run the colony for the next seventeen years.

Stuyvesant was not exactly a beloved leader. But many observers at the time and since regarded him as an effective one. He expanded the zone of settlement of New Amsterdam, strengthened its defenses and acquired more territory. He was also a skillful political infighter who recognized complexity even as he took firm stances, particularly in the realm of religion, where he resisted tolerance in favor of his own faith tradition of the Dutch Reformed Church.[8]

But there were limits to Stuyvesant's reach. In particular, relations with the English were tricky: both powers were Protestant and had shared enemies in Catholic Spain and France, each of which controlled large American empires. But while often allied and even friendly, English settlement vastly outnumbered that of the Dutch. Encroachment and economic competition were common, even as the Dutch tolerated English settlement in what the West India Company considered Dutch turf on Long Island. Through careful diplomacy, Stuyvesant was able to secure the Treaty of Hartford in 1650, which established clear borders between the New Netherland and New England in Connecticut (near Greenwich) and on Long Island (at Oyster Bay).

Having secured his northern frontier, Stuyvesant and his colleagues at the West India Company turned their attention south. Stuyvesant had hoped to open up Dutch trade in the Caribbean, but the English blocked those routes.[9] New Sweden also became increasingly worrisome. In the decade after its founding, the colony had consolidated—a development all the more galling for the role of Dutch money and figures like Minuit. Despite such tensions, the two nations collaborated in the early 1640s to expel a group of English settlers who were laying claim to the area. New Sweden generally prospered under the leadership of John Printz (1643–53), who built fortifications, established settlements and cultivated good relations with the local Indigenous people, most of whom were farmers rather than hunters. Once Stuyvesant came to power, he challenged Printz's sovereignty whenever he could. New Sweden's imperial health waned in the early 1650s, as the Swedish government neglected its support, which allowed Stuyvesant to establish Fort Casimir in modern-day New Castle, Delaware, giving the Dutch more control over both sides of South River traffic. Printz responded to his difficulties by assuming a more authoritarian approach, which alienated settlers, leading to his departure and replacement by a new governor, Johan Rising, in 1654.[10]

Rising arrived in New Sweden with a ship full of supplies and settlers and an ambition to press these advantages against the Dutch. He launched a successful attack on Fort Casimir—he renamed it Fort Trinity in honor of the Church holiday of Trinity Sunday when it was taken—and re-established Swedish control over the South River. He also recruited more settlers to come from Europe, boosting the colony's population from a dangerously low seventy to well almost four hundred.[11] Among the inhabitants of New Sweden were a group of Finns who came to New Sweden by way of the mother country and whose distinctive style of home construction—log cabins—diffused across the continent in centuries to come. By the mid-seventeenth century, New Sweden, whose flat landscape, diffuse settlement

TREE HOUSE: Recreation of the New Sweden Governor John Printz's cabin in Salem. He ran the colony between 1643 and 1653. *Jim Cullen*.

and river traffic made it culturally as well as geographically distinct from the cluster of European settlement centered on New Amsterdam, was gaining momentum. But in 1654, disease and famine stalled it.

This was the moment Stuyvesant, at the urging of the New Amsterdam business community, decided to strike. The first in what would be a series of Anglo-Dutch wars ended somewhat inconclusively in 1654 with minor Dutch concessions. More serious was a defeat in Brazil at the hands of the Portuguese. The Dutch decided to regroup by reinvesting in New Netherland, sending troops and ships to New Amsterdam. Stuyvesant used this opportunity to launch an expedition to attack New Sweden. In the summer of 1655, an armada of ships and men left Sandy Hook and sailed south, rounding Cape May and heading up the South River. He anchored between two Swedish forts on either side of the river, cutting off communication

STRATEGIC LOCATIONS: Site of Fort Casimir/Trinity, New Castle, a stronghold for control of the Delaware River. NJ/DE Memorial Bridge is in the distance. *Jim Cullen*.

between them. Stuyvesant then dispatched a messenger to the closer of the two with a demand for unconditional surrender—"restitution of our property," as he put it.[12]

The Swedes were caught flat-footed. They sent an emissary named Von Elswick to negotiate; given the panoply of languages spoken at the scene, they conducted negotiations, such as they were, in Latin. Von Elswick realized he had little choice but admit defeat. "Today it's me," he told Stuyvesant. "Tomorrow it will be you." Stuyvesant ignored the jibe and moved quickly to assert control over the colony. Recognizing its future lay in more settlement—the Dutch were at a disadvantage relying on trade to the degree they did—he invited the Finns to stay. As would many of the Swedes.[13]

Stuyvesant's victory did not come without cost, however. In September 1655—before he returned from his expedition—an alliance of six hundred Indigenous peoples launched an attack on lower Manhattan in solidarity with the Swedes. This attack was followed by a series of others across the Hudson in what is now Hackensack and Hoboken. The Dutch believed that the attack was actually a reprisal for a Dutchman killing an Indigenous woman for stealing peaches, which is why the conflict was dubbed the Peach

RESIDENTIAL DEVELOPMENT: Re-created log cabin in Swedesboro. These structures were built by Finnish settlers in New Sweden and spread rapidly across the continent. *Wikimedia Commons*.

War. But it was in fact an organized act revenge, one that took weeks for the Dutch to defeat. In its aftermath, Stuyvesant negotiated the repurchase of land between the Hudson and Hackensack Rivers and founded the settlement of Bergen.

By the mid-1650s, New Netherland was clearly growing in strength as well as in its borders, which ran the length of modern New Jersey. With its relatively light trading regulations and concentration of financial talent, the Dutch West India Company headquarters of New Amsterdam was rapidly emerging as an international mercantile crossroads in the North Atlantic, an identity that would only grow in centuries to come. But the rising profile of New Netherland was also a problem: it had become an asset ripe for the picking. Stuyvesant knew this; as two of his biographers noted, the English threat and the Peach War convinced him that "the trading-post status of New Netherland would not achieve security or permanence for the colony. Walls and forts and soldiers for defense were needed—not traders, but farmers; not peddlers, but carpenters—to build the colony and maintain it."[14] His challenge was convincing the rest of the colony and his Dutch patrons, who relished a society founded on diversity, aspiration and economic gain.

And so it was that Stuyvesant was powerless when an English fleet sailed into New Amsterdam in the spring of 1664 demanding that the Dutch turn over control of the colony. Stuyvesant desperately exhorted his countrymen to resist, but the will wasn't there, in part because the English offered terms that made their invasion more like a corporate merger than a military occupation (in truth, it was both). Stuyvesant sent a lawyer to sign articles of capitulation, and New Netherland was renamed New York (New Amsterdam also became New York City) in honor of the English duke who would soon become King James II.

This wasn't quite the end of New Netherland. In the complex jockeying of the Anglo-Dutch wars, the Dutch succeeded in retaking Manhattan in 1673, but it was dealt back to the English as part of a complex set of trades at the bargaining table the following year. From that point on, the region was English in governance, even if it remained strongly Dutch in character.

Meanwhile the Duke of York broke off the southern part of his new acquisition and granted it to two allies, Sir George Carteret and John Lord Berkeley, creating the new entity of New Jersey. Berkeley sold his share, resulting in a split into two colonies—East Jersey and West Jersey, which were eventually reunited in 1702.

After the first fall of New Amsterdam, Stuyvesant returned to the Netherlands to make a report to the government. But he subsequently went back to America, settling in Manhattan. In the decades that followed, the Dutch population of the colony continued to grow and spread. Amid the upheaval of the insurrection that followed the overthrow of James II known as Leisler's Rebellion, Dutch families moved from New York into the area between the Hackensack and Raritan Rivers.[15] There they mingled with English, Scottish, Swedish, Susquehannock and Lenape populations as part of the diverse demographic landscape that has been central to the character of New Jersey ever since.

Today, the Dutch legacy in New Jersey is faint, most obviously evident in place names like Pavonia, Paulus Hook and Arthur Kill (*kill* is the Dutch word for "river"). But it is nevertheless more prominent that that of New Sweden, which Stuyvesant succeeded in wiping off the map of what was once called the New World. Of course, the Swedes were not the only losers in the struggle to control the continent. Even for the winners, dominion is temporary. The British were defeated by the Americans, who have controlled New Jersey for a quarter of a millennium. It remains to be seen how much longer that will last.

2

REVEREND EDWARDS KEEPS THE FAITH AT PRINCETON

A FIERY PURITAN TAKES REFUGE BEYOND THE BORDERS OF NEW ENGLAND

The arrival of the visiting minister on May 28, 1747, was not terribly surprising. After all, hosting travelers was part of the job for the pastor of the Congregational Church in Northampton, Massachusetts. This particular arrival, David Brainerd, most recently of Cranbury, New Jersey, was eager to spend time in the home of Reverend Jonathan Edwards, a man he regarded as a mentor—and the most famous clergyman in America. Unfortunately, Brainerd was not well: he was afflicted with the disease we now know as tuberculosis. He spent four months trying to recover at the Edwards home, cared for by Edwards's daughter Jerusha. The two would form a close bond, and indeed in the years that followed there would be much speculation about where their relationship was headed. But Brainerd died that fall; Jerusha, afflicted with a sudden fever, perished a few months later.[16] The grief-stricken Reverend Edwards would find solace, as he so often did, in his writing, producing a tribute to his protégé in the book that became *The Life of David Brainerd*. It was one of the most famous works of religious literature for the next hundred years, a foundational text for generations of missionaries.

Edwards's relationship with Brainerd, and the book he wrote about him, would have another important legacy as well. It cemented Edwards's ties with a group of renegade ministers who had just established a college in New Jersey. His contacts with these reformers would intensify personally and professionally in the coming years, and Edwards would become the president of that college a decade later, solidifying its standing as an important educational institution. We know it as Princeton.

In the eighteenth century, North America was a land of empires—The French and Spanish claimed huge swaths of territory, as did the powerful Iroquois Confederacy in the northeastern part of the continent and Comancheria in the southwest.[17] And then, of course, there was the most populous empire of all: that of the British, which stretched from Maine to Georgia. Any tract of land that large was likely to be culturally diverse, and indeed, there were clear regional differences in the New England, Middle and Southern colonies. But there were also important differences *within* those regions. And in that era, no differences were more important than religious ones. Indeed, there were sometimes important differences even within the same Christian denominations.

Such intra-religious differences were especially fraught in New England. In part, that's because the region was settled by religious dissidents—notably the Pilgrims of Plymouth and the Puritans of Massachusetts, which ultimately absorbed Plymouth in 1691. Perhaps it's not surprising that fiercely committed religious activists would quarrel among themselves over issues of doctrine, which is what happened with the founding of Connecticut (originally the two separate colonies of Hartford and New Haven) as well as Rhode Island. Harvard was founded in 1636 to train ministers, and Yale followed in 1701 because its founders didn't think Harvard was rigorous enough. Still, whatever quarrels the faithful may have had with each other, there were plenty of other threats to keep them relatively united, and however negatively they may have

Godly: Jonathan Edwards (1703–1758). The New England theologian put the College of New Jersey (Princeton) on the map when he accepted its presidency. *Wikimedia Commons*.

viewed one another—or the official Church of England, against which they all rebelled—*nothing* could ever be as bad as Roman Catholicism, led by a pope they considered the Antichrist. But ethnically speaking, New England was the most homogeneous region in British North America, and compared with other colonies, it was religiously homogeneous as well.

This was decidedly not the case in the colony of New Jersey. At different points, its territory had been tussled over by Dutch, Swedish and English settlers, all of whom who brought their religious traditions with them. All of these nations were Protestant, but the Dutch, who had fought a long war of independence with Spain, were committed to religious tolerance, which meant that small pockets of Catholics and Jews were permitted to settle there. All of these faiths persisted once the British took over in the late seventeenth century. But now distinctly English sects were added to the mix, among them the Church of England and the Puritan tradition of New England, which was particularly prominent in the northern part of the colony—or, as it was known at the time, East Jersey.[18]

Puritanism was a religious tradition with a series of varieties, all of which were united under the doctrines of the French-born Swiss theologian John Calvin, who emphasized the doctrine of predestination, one emphasizing that individuals could not determine on their own whether or not they would achieve salvation. To think otherwise—to think you could know, buy or otherwise transact yourself into God's good graces—was to embrace corruption of the kind that had led to Martin Luther to protest against the corrupt Catholic Church and trigger the Reformation in 1517.

In Massachusetts, the dominant variety of Puritanism was Congregationalism, a term that referred to the fact that each church was an independent entity. But another variant, Presbyterianism, was organized on larger units of churches known as presbyteries, and it was this tradition in particular that took root in New Jersey. (The Church of England was organized on the still larger unit of episcopacies, which is why the Church of England became known as the Episcopal Church after the American Revolution; it was particularly strong in the southern colonies.) By the early eighteenth century, the line between Congregationalists and Presbyterians had become relatively porous. Certainly, there were more important things for the heirs of the Puritans to fight about, such as whether the minister of your church had really and truly given himself over to Christ.

In a general sense, this was the great drama of Puritanism in America: since you could never really know whether or not you were destined for heaven—and your confidence that you *were* saved might be a form of arrogance or self-deception—committed believers always had to question their motives. They had to offer convincing testimony of their conversion from sin to salvation in order to become members of a church and remain vigilant in their lives that they were doing the right things for the right reasons. So it was all the more important that the clergy who led these churches were themselves convincing models of piety—because, as everyone knew, Satan could work in devious ways.

As one might imagine, religious life of this kind could be exhausting (and it helps explain why many colonists drifted away from the old faith). But it could also be very exciting, as moments of shame and fear jostled with others of great joy—and, at times, excitement—when one experienced the force of irresistible grace suddenly surging into their lives. This excitement could be all the more powerful when it was experienced collectively in periodic "awakenings" that could sweep through churches, regions and even nations. In British America, one such surge, known as the First Great Awakening, erupted in the 1730s, and Reverend Jonathan Edwards was determined to make the most of it.

Edwards was, if one can speak of people who had overthrown the monarchy in the English Civil War a century earlier, a kind of Puritan royalty. His grandfather Solomon Stoddard was the pastor of the Congregational Church of Northampton, Massachusetts, and known as the "Pope of the Connecticut Valley." His father, Timothy Edwards, was also a well-known pastor based in Windsor, Connecticut, which is where his son Jonathan was born in 1703. Jonathan Edwards was a child with a prodigious intellect who entered Yale when he was thirteen years old. in addition to his studies of religion, was also deeply committed to the study of science, which he regarded as a means of understanding the wonders of God's working in the world. Thus it was that he read the work of Isaac Newton and wrote a famous, closely observed analysis of a spider.[19] After a stint of service as a young minister in New York City, Edwards was called to take over the ministry of his grandfather in Northampton when Solomon Stoddard died in 1729.

By most accounts, Edwards was a popular and successful pastor in Northampton. But his ministry took on a whole new level of intensity with the arrival of the First Great Awakening there in the mid-1730s. Edwards tended his flock on a local level, but he also wrote an account of what he was seeing, *A Faithful Narrative in the Surprising Work of God in the Conversion of Many Hundred Souls in Northampton*, in 1737, which made him famous in

Great Britain and America (he developed a particularly devoted following in Scotland). Edwards's 1741 sermon "Sinners in the Hands of an Angry God," with its unforgettable image of a spider dangling over the edge of a fire, remains a classic expression of the horrors of damnation coupled with the redemptive power of God's unconditional love.[20] Over the course of the next two decades, he became a prolific and influential defender of the Awakening and its legacy.

But this was complicated. The initial wave of the First Great Awakening was met with widespread acclaim, and it was taken to a whole new level when the Reverend George Whitefield—the rock star of American evangelism—crisscrossed the Atlantic in his periodic tours through North America, which included stops in New Jersey. But Whitefield sometimes stirred resentment among other ministers and aligned himself with what became a faction of "New Lights," who emphasized the importance of visible piety and intensity in preaching, in contrast to Old Lights who maintained more traditional ways and who warned that emotional displays were not necessarily clear signs of salvation. The fight between New Lights and Old Lights was particularly intense at Yale, where radical young students like David Brainerd clashed with the Puritan establishment. Brainerd, who was heard to utter a dismissive comment about a member of the faculty there, was expelled. He nevertheless remained committed to his faith and began working as a missionary among the Lenape people of New Jersey.

The New Lights were in a very literal sense antiestablishment, but they were not without resources. One of their key leaders was Gilbert Tennant, whose famous sermon "The Dangers of an Unconverted Ministry" became a classic statement of protest against an old guard that clung to its privilege and power at the expense of its commitment to the faith.[21] Back in 1727, Tennant's father, Reverend William Tennant, established the Log College, a modest Presbyterian seminary in Neshinamy, Pennsylvania, just outside Philadelphia. In 1746, the Tennants and their allies, who had ordained David Brainerd after he got kicked out of Yale, established the College of New Jersey in Elizabeth. In 1747, the college, whose president Jonathan Dickinson had died suddenly, moved its operations to Newark, under the leadership the Reverend Aaron Burr (a name that may sound familiar, for reasons to be explained later).

And where was Jonathan Edwards amid all these developments? The short answer: in a tricky position. Edwards was a true believer in the Great Awakening and indeed had become its primary theorist, even as Whitefield

BURR IN THE SADDLE: Reverend Aaron Burr Sr. (1716–1757). He married Jonathan Edwards's daughter Esther; their son became a notorious Founding Father (see chapter 4). *Wikimedia Commons.*

became its star performer. (The two men admired each other, though Whitefield was friendlier with the far less pious Benjamin Franklin.)[22] Like the Tennants, Edwards also believed there was danger in an unconverted ministry. But he was also a prominent member of a powerful religious establishment and not fully comfortable with the proto-democratic thrust of the New Light movement. In his biography of Brainerd, for example, Edwards noted that David Brainerd had shown all too human "heats of imagination, intemperate zeal, or spiritual pride" deserving of punishment. But he nevertheless loved and honored this man who did truly holy work.[23] Edwards was also an ally of Tennant and Burr—his daughter would marry Reverend Burr and move to Newark—and he would visit New Jersey periodically. *Ideologically*, Edwards staked out a maverick stance. But *temperamentally*, he was a conservative at heart. This was a volatile combination at a volatile time.

And so it was that at the very moment the College of New Jersey was getting underway, Edwards faced the great crisis of his career. As is so often the case, this began as a fairly trivial matter that snowballed over time. In March 1744, Edwards was concerned to learn that a group of young men had been passing around books on medicine and midwifery in a prurient manner. He brought them up on discipline charges, issuing a call for a list of suspects and witnesses that did not distinguish between the two. In the proceedings that followed, there was a widespread sense that he was coming down too hard on them—that he was too Puritanical—and while the men ultimately apologized, there was a grudging and limited quality to their capitulation. The perception of Edwards's harshness was compounded by awkward negotiations about his salary, which was paid out of town tax revenues. Edwards had always been fairly well liked in Northampton, even if he was never exactly charismatic. But now there was a sense of stiffness associated with him that would be hard to shake.[24]

Edwards compounded this perception in a much more serious matter shortly after Brainerd's and his daughter's deaths, which was followed by the death of John Stoddard, the brother of his grandfather Solomon, from whom Edwards had inherited his pastorate. Solomon Stoddard had always maintained a relatively low barrier of entry in his church, concerned with keeping its membership numbers up. But in 1749, Edwards announced more stringent standards for who would be able to receive communion, a reversal of policy that went over badly. In early 1750, Edwards's ministry was brought up for a vote for removal, which he lost. The lion of the Great Awakening was out of a job.

But not for long. In 1751, Edwards accepted a ministry in Stockbridge, Massachusetts. This was a missionary town in which Edwards was to tend to a mixed-race community of English and Mahican people and an opportunity do the kind of work for which he had celebrated David Brainerd's work in New Jersey. It was challenging—the Mahicans could be understandably skeptical of the efforts made on their behalf, especially given the way they were treated by British settlers, who coveted, and rapidly populated, their lands. The challenge was all the greater given the outbreak of the Seven Years' (also known as the French and Indian) War in 1754, which heightened racial and international tensions.

But this was also a time of notable productivity in Edward's literary career. It was in these years that he wrote some of his most important works, among them *Freedom of the Will* (1754) and *Original Sin* (1758), as well as the posthumously published *The Nature of True Virtue* (1765).[25] In these and other books, Edwards affirmed the power and relevance of the Great Awakening while articulating powerful intellectual opposition to the doctrine of Arminianism (named after the Dutch theologian Jacobus Arminius, who championed the role of free will in a Puritan context). Edwards questioned where those who thought they had free choice got that idea, which he argued was *itself* a product divine design. He also drew on modern notions of scientific order that he attributed to God's will, which did include an element of choice that elided the grimly mechanistic determinism that has haunted notions of science ever since.[26] So Edwards was a complex, cutting-edge thinker, even as he staked out tough-minded positions that embraced the Puritan tradition.

But in Massachusetts, at least, Edwards was swimming against the cultural tides. One of his strongest allies had been the governor of the colony, Jonathan Belcher. But Belcher had been removed from his post in 1741, and six years later he became the governor of New Jersey, where Edwards visited him on a number of occasions. Belcher, who disliked an Anglican establishment that was increasingly prevalent in the British colonies, was a classic Puritan Congregationalist with strong ties to the College of New Jersey. Belcher threw his weight behind moving the institution from Newark to Princeton, donating his sizable library to the school and fundraising for the construction of Nassau Hall, named for King William III (1689–1702), who hailed from the Dutch house of Nassau and championed religious liberty. The large stone edifice became the flagship building of what was now an inter-denominational institution when it was completed in 1756.

Edwards's son-in-law Aaron Burr, married to his daughter Esther, continued in his role as president after the move. But when Burr died suddenly in 1757, the trustees moved quickly to offer the job to Edwards. He hesitated, worried about teaching and administrative responsibilities that might interfere with his commitment to writing. Reassured on these points, he accepted the post and moved down to Princeton to join his daughter with the intention that the rest of his family would follow. Edwards enjoyed spending time with his grandson Aaron Burr Jr., who was nineteenth months old at the time and just beginning to talk. His

TOWERING: Nassau Hall, erected 1754. The largest stone building in the thirteen colonies, it became the flagship building of Princeton University. *Wikimedia Commons*.

FAMILY PLOTS: Jonathan Edwards was buried in Princeton cemetery the year following its founding in 1757. His grandson Aaron Burr occupies an adjacent grave site. *Wikimedia Commons.*

mother described him as "very sly and mischievous,"[27] a description that would prove prophetic.

Edwards was officially installed as the president of the College of New Jersey on February 16, 1758. Two weeks later, committed to modern scientific approaches to public health, he underwent inoculation for smallpox, that scourge of human life for thousands of years that could scar or kill those afflicted with it. (George Washington survived a bout of smallpox; Benjamin Franklin, whose brother James ridiculed vaccination, lost a son to the disease, which had also killed College of New Jersey founder Jonathan Dickinson in 1746.) Unfortunately, the serum that was injected into Edwards was infected, and he died on March 12.[28] The tragedy was compounded by the death of his daughter Esther a few weeks later and his wife, Sarah, a few months after that, leaving his grandchildren as orphans. But the Edwards legacy, stretched to its breaking point, nevertheless survived.

AS MANY OBSERVERS HAVE noted, Edwards was a man of another time. This is of course true of all people in the past, but in his case, it seems particularly relevant to say so because he was the defender of a faith that was embattled for much of his career and would continue to recede, even in its heartland of New England, in the decades after his death. In this regard, Princeton was something of an asylum for Edwards—a New Jersey outpost of Puritanism that held fast to the core doctrines of its theology. As his most recent and magisterial biographer, George Marsden, noted, Edwards in the Massachusetts of the 1740s was asking his congregation to behave like a Puritan community in the 1640s, and that simply was no longer in the cards.[29] And yet Edwards was clear-eyed about where the logic of self-determination would lead: an intensifying tendency toward questioning authority (religious and otherwise) that would lead not only toward rebellion (political and otherwise) but also a drift away from faith itself, with consequences that might seem superficially liberating but psychically unsettling and even desolating.

Edwards's death was certainly a blow to the College of New Jersey, which aspired not simply to be a factory for producing ministers but a more general institution of higher learning that could compete with its peers in New England. Edwards's grandson Aaron Burr would graduate from the college in 1772 and go on to a career as an officer in the American Revolution and as a lawyer in New York City with his friendly rival Alexander Hamilton, with whom he could plausibly claim a status as a Founding Father. (For more on Burr, see chapter 4.) His classmate James Madison, class of 1771, went on to become the chief architect of the U.S. Constitution and the nation's fourth president. In the decades that followed, the College of New Jersey became a favored pipeline for generations of southerners seeking to cement their place in the nation's elite.[30] Many of them came from families that enslaved African Americans, as indeed had Edwards himself, a practice he did not regard as incompatible with the tenets of Christianity, which did not insist on social equality in secular life even as it did as a matter of Christian charity and the equality of all souls in the eyes of God.

The College of New Jersey was renamed Princeton University in 1896 (see chapter 8) and is now routinely named as one of the most powerful and prestigious institutions of higher learning in the world. In its broad-based commitment to reforming the world and bringing it ever closer to an unattainable perfectibility, it continues the mission of its founders, notably Edwards, one of the most powerful minds America ever produced.

3

GENERAL WASHINGTON FOILS FAILURE IN FREEHOLD

A FOUNDING FATHER SEIZES THE INITIATIVE—AGAIN—AND NEVER LOOKS BACK

New Jersey made George Washington.

This may sound like an odd thing to say. George Washington was not from New Jersey, and he spent relatively little of his life there. While he did lead his beloved Continental army to a few victories in New Jersey during the American Revolution—the National Park Service, among others, calls it "the crossroads of the Revolution"[31]—the significance of these battles pales when compared with the triumph in his home state of Virginia at the Battle of Yorktown in 1781. Moreover, Washington's career was more than a military one; he was active in colonial politics before the Revolution, and he served as president of the Constitutional Convention of 1787 in Philadelphia before assuming the presidency as the nation's first chief executive in New York City two years later. More often than not, New Jersey was a place Washington passed *through*, one of the many places he slept, rather than a focal point for his attention or achievement.

But literally and figuratively, New Jersey was more central to Washington's life and legend than may initially appear. During the Revolution, he spent more time there with the Continental army than any other state, including the winters of 1776–77, 1778–79 and 1779–80.[32] More fundamentally, New Jersey was the crucible of his career. When Washington brought the Continental army into New Jersey in the fall of 1776, he led a bedraggled force on the cusp of destruction. A year later, his fitness to remain in charge

Charged: Washington enters the fray at the Battle of Monmouth, showing great bravery and averting disaster. *Wikimedia Commons.*

was openly questioned by his peers and by key leaders of the Continental Congress in Philadelphia. But when Washington fought his final battle in New Jersey in Freehold at the Battle of Monmouth Courthouse in June 1778—the longest day of combat in the Revolution[33]—he did so as the unquestioned leader of a professional fighting force with the strength and resilience to finally defeat the greatest imperial army in the world. After Monmouth, Washington never looked back on his road to greatness.

It's worth considering how he got there.

The first half of 1776 was a time of anxiety but also achievement and hope for the Patriots of the American Revolution. Massachusetts militias had successfully stood up to British Regulars at the Battles of Lexington, Concord and Bunker Hill in 1775, catalyzing a nascent nationalist movement. It was John Adams, a key figure in Massachusetts politics and a representative at the First and Second Continental Congresses, who had nominated George Washington, one of the few rebel leaders with military experience, to be the Virginian leader of what was then a largely New England army so as to emphasize the truly continental span of the revolutionary movement.[34] Washington arrived in Boston in the summer of 1775 to take over what was aspirationally called the Continental army and skillfully supervised the fortification of Dorchester Heights overlooking the city, forcing the British to evacuate in March 1776. That July, Congress issued the Declaration of Independence, a manifesto meant to be a turning point in the history of the world, as indeed it became.

It was all downhill from there in the second half of 1776. Even as the Founding Fathers were putting the finishing touches on the Declaration, the largest invasion force ever assembled in the Western Hemisphere was landing in New York. Washington anticipated this but made a series of mistakes that almost proved fatal. He was thoroughly outmaneuvered at the Battle of Long Island and only escaped complete destruction because a deep fog on the night of August 27 allowed his army to escape across the East River. He compounded his mistake by staying in Manhattan—another island trap he managed to escape—but not before deciding to attempt a hopeless defense of the Hudson River from twin forts, Fort Washington and Fort Lee, on either side. He lost both by mid-November, brought his army into New Jersey and spent the next six weeks in steady retreat from one end of the state to the other, not stopping until he crossed the Delaware River into Pennsylvania. It was on this retreat through New Jersey that Thomas Paine wrote the first installment of what became his famous pamphlet *The American Crisis*, which begins with the line "These are the times that try men's souls."[35]

Washington, who needed to keep a brave face in public, was more candid in private. "Such is my situation that if I were to wish the bitterest curse to an enemy, I should put in him in my stead," he wrote to his cousin Lund in September, while still in Manhattan. "I see the impossibility of serving with reputation, or doing any essential service to the cause by continuing in command, and yet I am told that if I quit the command inevitable ruin will follow from the distraction that will ensue. In confidence I tell you that I never was in such an unhappy, divided state since I was born." By year's end, when he was in Trenton, Washington's mood had not improved. "I think the game is pretty much near up," he told his brother Samuel on December 18.[36]

Nor did his new surroundings offer much in the way of hope. "New Jersey was not a good place to be during the American Revolution," noted the state's premier historian of the period, Maxine Lurie.[37] Unlike New England, where support for the rebel cause burned bright and the population was culturally homogenous in terms of religion and ethnicity, New Jersey was an ethnographically diverse state sandwiched between two colonial giants, New York and Pennsylvania, both with large Loyalist factions. The population of New Jersey contained anti-war Quakers (and some pro-war ones) as well as residents of Dutch, Swedish and German descent, and 8 percent of its population was African American. Their stance on the war could be hard to predict amid often shifting circumstances. Though Patriots had seized control of the new state's governmental machinery by 1776—ousting William Franklin, the Loyalist son of Benjamin Franklin, who was not on speaking terms with his son—partisan warfare, intimidation and theft were facts of life for the entire war. Recent scholarship has emphasized the degree to which the American Revolution was a civil war, and New Jersey offers a particularly vivid example of this truism.[38]

British brothers Admiral Richard Howe and General William Howe, who had lost a brother who fought alongside colonists in in the French and Indian War, considered themselves friends of the Americans. When they arrived in New York in July 1776, they issued a proclamation offering "free and general pardon" to all those willing to sign an oath to the Crown. An estimated 2,700 New Jerseyans took the pledge in the months that followed with a range of enthusiasm that ran from explicit fervor to pragmatic calculation. (One such figure, Richard Stockton, captured that November, became the only person to sign the Declaration of Independence who also signed the oath, though he disavowed it upon his release and was accepted back into the cause in good standing.) Early the following year, Washington followed with an order of his own, allowing those "influenced by inimical motives, intimidated by the threats of the enemy or deluded by the Proclamation" to recant. All of this shows how tangled and unclear the state's fate was in those months following the nation's founding announcement.[39]

As he reeled across the state, Washington's primary strategic objective—as it would be for so much of the war—was keeping his army intact to fight another day. But he was also mindful that as a matter of politics as well as military morale he could not remain on the defensive indefinitely. "As nothing but necessity obliged me to retire before the Enemy, & leave so much of the Jerseys unprotected [Washington refers to the old distinction between East Jersey, oriented toward New York, and West Jersey, oriented toward Pennsylvania], I conceive it as my duty, and it corresponds with my Inclination to make head against them as soon as there shall be the least probability of doing so with propriety," he told Continental Congress president John Hancock on December 5.[40]

This is why, with an audacity that would occasionally surface in a temperament whose default setting was caution, Washington made the bold decision to cross over the Delaware River from his base in Pennsylvania

BY GEORGE: Washington at the Battle of Trenton. A pinprick victory, but the first in a series of offensives in New Jersey. *Library of Congress.*

and lead a surprise attack on Trenton on the night of December 25, 1776, an event immortalized in the famous 1851 painting by Emanuel Leutze. Here he achieved complete surprise in defeating a largely mercenary force of German Hessians before retreating back across the river. This would be the first stroke in a series of events now known as the "Ten Crucial Days" that would feature a similarly counterintuitive forward movement and stand at Assunpink Creek (also known as the Second Battle of Trenton) on January 2, which Washington was able to wage and win after persuading soldiers whose enlistments were expiring to stay with him a little longer. He then followed it up with yet another offensive at Princeton the following day, continuing a pattern of Patriot energy. These moves led the British to pull out the region, heading for the relative safety of New York, and allowed Washington to set up his winter quarters as Morristown, where the Continental army remained until the following spring. As a result, New Jersey swung in a Patriot direction, even if partisan warfare continued.[41]

It's important to be clear about what these victories did, and didn't, represent. Washington and his troops had demonstrated a resilience and resourcefulness that showed the Revolution would not be ending anytime soon. But militarily speaking, victories at Trenton and Princeton were the equivalent of a punch in the nose: shocking and painful, but not really decisive. What the Americans really needed was to land a punch in the gut—a blow to the solar plexus that would knock the British down, changing the character of the conflict.

They got it—but the triumph was not in New Jersey, and it was not Washington's. And that was a problem.

IN SURVEYING THE NORTH American continent in early 1777, the British high command saw two major opportunities to bring the rebels to their knees in the coming campaign season. The first was to lead an army under the command of Major General John Burgoyne from Montreal down the Hudson River toward New York City, a move that held the promise of cutting off New England—the most radical region of the rebellion—from the rest of the colonies. The second was for the Howe brothers to lead a joint expedition from their base in New York to capture the Patriot capital of Philadelphia, the largest city in the Western Hemisphere and nerve center of the rebellion. Through a series of misunderstandings and competing agendas, the British decided to pursue both objectives simultaneously. This meant that Burgoyne would not be getting the help from the Howes when he moved south. It was one in a series of cascading miscues that culminated at the Battle of Saratoga, in which the Americans forced the surrender of Burgoyne's entire army. This was an astounding victory in itself. But it was even more momentous in that it convinced a previously skeptical French government that the American Revolution was a good investment for an empire seeking to take its greatest rival down a peg. France declared war on Great Britain and entered a military alliance with the United States. The victory at Saratoga raised the profile of the American commanding general Horatio Gates, who got crucial help (not fully recognized) from General Benedict Arnold, who was wounded at the battle—and nursed grievances that would ultimately result in his switching sides three years later.

Meanwhile, back in New Jersey, Washington was relieved that the Howes were not moving to reinforce Burgoyne, as he was terrified by the prospect of seeing the new nation cut in two. But he was uncertain how General William Howe would move into Pennsylvania. As it turned out, Howe decided to rely on his brother Richard to ferry British troops from Sandy Hook to present-day Elkton, Maryland, wheeling around to attack Philadelphia from the south. Washington, who tracked British forces by land moving south from

Morristown, was soundly defeated at the Battle of Brandywine, Pennsylvania, on September 11, leaving the road open to Philadelphia. Washington sent General Anthony Wayne in a failed bid to prevent British capture of the city at the Battle of Paoli on September 20. After it fell, Washington tried a Trenton-style surprise counterattack on British forces on the Philadelphia suburb of Germantown on October 4. But it didn't work this time. Badly bruised, undersupplied and leaking men, the Continental army proceeded to nearby Valley Forge to reorganize and take stock of what was now a complex strategic situation of major victories, serious defeats and a French ally who was powerful, self-interested and unpredictable in terms of where and how it would strike a blow against the British.

It was a to be a long winter. Valley Forge has been rightly remembered as the psychic and logistical crucible of the American Revolution, an interlude where a fighting force on the verge of disintegration struggled to hold on and rebuild itself. It did so, thanks in part to the arrival of the first French supplies, tenuous but successful recruitment efforts and the arrival of a Prussian officer, Baron Friedrich von Steuben (an invented title, but an accepted one), who supervised the drilling of the troops into a more professional army.

In all this, Washington's leadership—and example—were vital. He cajoled Congress for money, put talented people in leadership positions (like Rhode Islander Nathanael Greene, who was appointed quartermaster) and endured privations alongside his men, even if Washington was nobody's idea of one of the guys. Though Washington valued the role of local militia in the war—the New Jersey forces led by Philemon Dickinson would prove to be particularly valuable—he lobbied hard for a national force with longer enlistments and made progress on this front.[42]

But for Washington himself, the fall of 1777 and winter of 1778 was personally challenging because for the first time in his career, his competence was being openly challenged—and by people in a position to do something about it. The carping had started as early as June, when Congressional delegate Samuel Adams of Massachusetts criticized Washington's caution in New Jersey at the start of the Philadelphia campaign, calling for more "decisive" leadership and "a more enterprising spirit." Notwithstanding his role in getting Washington his job, Adams's cousin John was even more critical, asserting that Washington had lost the "masterly capacity" he had shown in Boston two years earlier.[43] (Adams spent much of his career envying Washington, his militancy conducted from a safe distance.) The grumbling grew in intensity after the defeats at Brandywine and Germantown, which appeared starker against the backdrop of the triumph at Saratoga. General Gates was being touted by some, inside and outside the army, as a replacement for Washington, talk Gates was happy to encourage. Washington had a particularly vocal, and indiscreet, critic in Thomas Conway, an Irishman formerly in the French army who was promoted to major general over Washington's objections. After a round of drinking, an aide to Gates showed an officer of Washington's a letter Conway had written in which he said of Gates, "Heaven has determined to save your country; or a weak General [that would be Washington] and bad Counselors would have ruined it." Washington dealt with such gossip—some of it rife at camp—with the disciplined restraint that had long been his trademark. When he received a copy of this letter, he coolly dispatched a note to Conway noting he had received it without further comment. The implication—I know what you're doing—was clear. Conway was reassigned to New York.[44]

A more nettlesome figure was the number-two figure in the Continental army, Charles Lee (the man for whom the borough of Fort Lee is named).[45] An experienced and talented officer in the British army whose pique over a lack of promotion led him to migrate to Virginia, Lee, a committed Patriot, had served with distinction in the early years of the war. But he grew increasingly impatient with his boss's leadership, some of which he expressed in letters to Washington's critics. In December 1776, commanding a force near Morristown, Lee was in the middle of defying Washington's orders to join him in New York when he was taken prisoner. He was paroled and rejoined the army at Valley Forge in the spring of 1778. Lee was accepted back into the fold, just in time for the coming campaign season, but showed a lack of tact in presenting Congress with a plan for reorganizing the army, one sharply at variance with Washington's ideas in Lee's emphasis on militias.[46]

For all the difficulties Washington faced at Valley Forge, the British were not without their own challenges, notwithstanding the relative comforts of occupied Philadelphia. Actually, this was one of the problems: the capture of the city did not have the damaging effect its occupiers had hoped it would. (The Continental Congress had relocated to the nearby city of York.) A bigger problem was the looming challenge of France: the rebels were wily ninety-pound weaklings, but the French were an eight-hundred-pound gorilla capable of inflicting real damage to British interests around the globe. It was well known that a large French fleet was on its way across the Atlantic in the spring of 1778. Was it headed for the plantation-rich British islands in the Caribbean? Could it overwhelm Admiral Howe and attack Philadelphia?

About the only thing that was clear to the British high command was that the army was in a vulnerable position in the City of Brotherly Love, especially because some of the troops there would be needed elsewhere.

By this point, there had been a change in command: General Howe headed back home, succeeded by his competent subordinate, Henry Clinton.[47] Clinton's orders were to relocate the army back to the safer environs of New York, a strategic retreat that would require logistical finesse while trying to minimize the implicit defeat in surrendering hard-won gains (and abandoning Tories who would be at the Patriots' mercy). In June 1778, Clinton began executing a long march across New Jersey.

The ball was now in Washington's court. Though he submitted the question of what to do to his officers for their ideas—which ranged from staying put to attacking New York—Washington was convinced he needed to take a measured initiative, as much for morale as for operational advantage. As his trusted protégé Greene put it, "People expect something of us."[48] And so once he determined that the British would be heading toward Sandy Hook, Washington led the Continental army back into New Jersey in hot pursuit of Clinton's army. At the end of June, he caught up with it in the town of Monmouth Court House, also known then (and more commonly now) as Freehold.[49] The town, near the center of the state, was a Patriot stronghold, its evocative name reflecting the aspirational notion of a community of egalitarian stakeholders. For the moment, though, it was to be a furnace of destruction amid a heat wave that sent temperatures in late June over one hundred degrees.

As per custom, Washington offered leadership of the attack to Lee, his ranking officer. But Lee, who believed that the plan was too aggressive, turned it town. Washington then entrusted the job to the young Marquis de Lafayette, a promising but still-green general who had gotten himself into trouble earlier that month in leading a foray against the British outside Philadelphia. Belatedly realizing he was forfeiting a chance for glory in leading what was to be a sizeable force, Lee changed course, offering a "thousand apologies" but requesting that "if this detachment does march that I may have command of it." Washington agreed. On June 28, he gave Lee a set of instructions—how specific they were would later be a matter of furious later dispute—to lead the assault, and Lee did so.[50]

Initially, the Battle of Monmouth Court House went well. But it soon became apparent that Lee was in over his head: he collided into a force that was much bigger than his was and one that was reinforced as Clinton's army turned to fight. Lee's men wilted from the heat and the onslaught, and as the day progressed there was serious danger the entire Continental line would crumple before Washington could commit the rest of his army to the fight.

Washington didn't realize how bad the situation had gotten until 1:00 p.m., when he sifted through reports from the field and realized a disaster was unfolding. At that point, he plunged into the fray, leading his troops toward Lee. When Washington found Lee, the angry commander-in-chief demanded to know "what was the meaning" of Lee's retreat, reputedly also calling him "a damned poltroon" (coward). Lee was shocked by the criticism. But both men recovered their composure, Lee taking Washington's cue to reform his line in a more defensible position while Washington himself took charge of the fight. Facing continuous danger from enemy fire, his presence "inspired universal ardour along the line," in the words of one officer. At that point, the engagement began to resemble the Battle of Bunker Hill, in that the British made multiple assaults and took heavy casualties. Washington had stemmed the tide. Many observers regard it as his finest hour as a battlefield commander.[51]

There was still a lot of fighting left to do that day, notably a long artillery barrage by each army that did little to change the strategic equation. By

HOME FRONT: The Rhea-Applegate house, one of three homes still standing from the 1778 Battle of Monmouth Courthouse in Freehold. *Wikimedia Commons*.

LEGENDARY: Twenty-three-year-old Mary Ludwig Hays accompanied her husband, William, at the Battle of Monmouth, where she was immortalized as "Molly Pitcher," who brought water to the troops and manned artillery. *Library of Congress*.

nightfall, both sides had been ground down to exhaustion. Clinton organized an overnight withdrawal and was gone by sunrise, leaving the field to Washington. On the other hand, Clinton successfully went ahead and did what he planned to all along: make his way to New York. Militarily speaking, the Battle of Monmouth Court House was a draw.

But the battle had more significance than that. Monmouth showed that Washington's army had grown in size, stature and experience, fighting a powerful enemy toe-to-toe on a large scale. Washington hadn't foiled Clinton's plans, but those plans were in themselves an acknowledgement of defeat: the British did not feel they could retain their gains of the previous year, and a war they had seemed on the cusp of winning was now turning into a stalemate. As indeed it would be for the next two years. The war had begun in New England in 1775–76 and moved into the mid-Atlantic in 1777–78. The British would try their luck in the South in 1780–81, and for a while, it looked like they might succeed. But by then Washington was finally able to coordinate his efforts with the French, fool the British into thinking that he was more obsessed with retaking New York than he actually was and win his most decisive victory of all at Yorktown.

The Freehold fight also had significant personal consequences for Washington. Historians have debated Lee's degree of culpability for what happened in the battle—recent scholarship suggests Washington was far too harsh on him[52]—but Lee's lack of social skills hurt him badly in the days that followed. Insulted by Washington's criticism, he demanded, and received, a court-martial. His indiscreet remarks, and the sustained hostility of Washington's staff, undercut Lee's case, and he was found guilty on three counts and suspended from the army for a year. (He was also involved in a duel dramatized in "Meet Me Inside," from the Broadway musical *Hamilton*.) "Here was another sense in which Washington won the Battle of Monmouth," historian Woody Holton has noted. "He rid himself of a second-in-command who had become a liability."[53] From this point forward, Washington's critics fell silent. He would spend the next nineteen years, to quote the title of a famous biography, as the new nation's "indispensable man."[54]

Here, then, is a compendium of greatness enacted in New Jersey: persistence, initiative, patience, tact and grace under pressure. The state was the crossroads of the Revolution, and it was also the crossroads of Washington's career. To be sure, he was only human: stiff and formal at times, with a temper he could not always control. He was also a man who enslaved hundreds of people. But Washington was unique among his peers in systematically seeking for years to emancipate them, something he finally achieved in his will amid resistance from his own family.[55] To call Washington a great man is to note the tension between the two words while holding fast to the former. He cleared a path to freedom through the Garden State.

4

VICE PRESIDENT BURR COMMITS MURDER IN WEEHAWKEN

A MYSTERIOUS FOUNDING FATHER FORFEITS HIS CAREER ON NATIVE GROUND

The most famous duel in American history—there were more of them than you might think—took place on a ledge of land directly across the Hudson River from contemporary 42nd Street in Manhattan, where, on July 11, 1804, Aaron Burr fatally shot one of the true giants of our nation's history: Alexander Hamilton. Like Hamilton, Burr was a transplanted New Yorker, one who, after service in the American Revolution, had come to the city to make his mark on the world. Hamilton had emigrated to New York from the Caribbean as a young man in a hurry. Burr's origins were closer to home: he was a native New Jerseyan. The colony of his birth was not simply a departure point but rather the site of some of the key moments in his life: Burr spent his childhood in Elizabeth, was educated at Princeton, fought at the Battle of Monmouth, met his beloved wife in Passaic and reached the turning point in his long and tumultuous life in Weehawken. He ranged far and wide over the course of a life that at different points took him to New England, Canada, the Ohio country and the Mississippi Territory—and then Europe. And yet for all this, though it's not exactly obvious or widely noted, the locus of Burr's life was, a little counterintuitively, northern New Jersey.

CLIFF-HANGER: Illustration of the New Jersey palisades at Weehawken. Monument at lower right indicates where the fateful Hamilton-Burr duel took place. *Wikimedia Commons.*

Actually, there was little about Burr's life that was intuitive. The son and grandson of famous ministers, he was notoriously amoral, even immoral, in the eyes of his contemporaries. Deeply immersed as he was in the controversies and policies of the early republic, it was never quite clear where Burr stood on the issues of his day (and it still isn't). An aristocrat with a feel for popular politics, he lived well but was perpetually in debt. Deeply devoted to his wife and daughter, he was also a notorious womanizer. An enslaver, he took care to educate his slaves (and advocated abolition). A relatively low-level New York politician, he came within a hair's breadth of snatching the presidency from Thomas Jefferson. A land speculator and mercenary, he may or may not have sought to lead a secessionist movement against the U.S. government. Your perspective on Burr is not simply a matter of who you ask, because they won't know for sure, either: Burr left behind few papers and wrote much of his correspondence in code.

But amid all these ambiguities, no event in Burr's life is more mystifying than his encounter with Alexander Hamilton on that hot July morning in 1804. What exactly was it that prompted their duel? What were Hamilton's intentions, and why was Burr so determined to resolve their conflict—

illegal in New Jersey, but less likely to be prosecuted than in New York— this way? How could the normally cool-headed Burr fail to understand the consequences of what would follow?

Amid these uncertainties, there are two things we know for sure. The first is that Aaron Burr was made in New Jersey. The second is that he was broken in New Jersey. He had experienced defeat in the years before Weehawken and would endure even more serious infamy after Weehawken. But Weehawken was his crucible, his point of no return. It is truly one of the most haunting crossroads of American history.

THE UNITED STATES HAS never had an official aristocracy, though plenty of Americans have had distinguished pedigrees. Some of these are a matter of Old World lineage; others inherited wealth over many generations (like the fabled Founding Families of Virginia—FFVs, as they were known). Aaron Burr, however, was the product of an aristocracy of talent. He descended from a New England ministry of the highest order, educated at a Yale founded because Harvard wasn't serious enough. Burr arrived in this world in the infancy of a Princeton founded to bring the empire of the mindful soul to New Jersey.

The really titanic figure in his ancestry was his maternal grandfather, the internationally famous Jonathan Edwards (1703–1758), who for many years presided over a powerful pulpit in Northampton, Massachusetts (see chapter 2). In 1752, Edwards's daughter, the highly intelligent and well-educated Esther, married Aaron Burr, a Presbyterian minister based in Newark, where he for many years had been working to establish a college in New Jersey. The couple had a daughter, Sally, born in 1754. In 1756, Burr relocated the college to the town of Princeton on the recommendation of Governor Jonathan Belcher and began organizing the construction of Nassau Hall, which was the largest building in North America at the time, and remains the signature structure of what we now call Princeton University.[56] It was also that year that Esther gave birth to Aaron Burr Jr. She described the experience as "gloomy" and called him "a little dirty noisy boy" who "requires a good Governor to bring him to terms," in marked contrast to his sister. Esther was nevertheless deeply attached to the child, especially after he unexpectedly survived serious illness as an infant.[57]

But a cascading series of disasters decimated the Burr family. They began when Aaron Burr Sr. came home from a trip to his father-in-law to tell him about an exciting religious revival at Princeton (he did so as the

French and Indian War was encroaching on the Edwards family, now based in Stockbridge, Massachusetts). He fell ill and died. At that point, Jonathan Edwards came down to Princeton to take over the presidency of the college for his son-in-law but perished after a botched smallpox vaccination. Then Esther got sick and died. Baby Aaron managed so survive another bout of illness, but when Edwards's wife, Sarah, came down from Massachusetts to tend to her grandchildren, she too fell fatally ill. In the space of about a year, the Burr children lost their mother, father and two grandparents. They would be raised by their uncle Timothy Edwards. As such, they were well-cared for, financially and otherwise (as well as they could be in household of fifteen other children), and the siblings remained close. But as a matter of love and loss, Burr's background was not unlike his future great rival Alexander Hamilton, whose childhood was marked by penury, uncertain patrimony and the loss of his own mother in childhood.[58]

Aaron Burr spent much of his childhood in Elizabethtown (now the city of Elizabeth). At age eleven, he applied for admission to Princeton but was turned down because he was too young. He spent the next two years studying and in 1769 applied again. This time he was accepted; though he sought to enter as a junior, he was admitted as a sophomore. Much younger than his peers, he was dubbed "Little Burr"—a statement as much about his stature as his age. (In this, too, Burr was like the diminutive Hamilton.) Burr was popular and made many lifelong friends, among them future New Jersey governor William Paterson and future president James Madison. Burr remained in Princeton for a while after he graduated in 1772. The text of the commencement address that he delivered, "Building Castles in the Air," has been lost. But the implicit critique of its title points to a pragmatism—critics would call it opportunism—that would characterize much of his subsequent life.[59]

Burr initially thought he would follow in his family's footsteps and become a minister, moving to central Connecticut to study. But he quickly decided that he would rather pursue law and began his studies in Litchfield County—right on the Massachusetts border—in the mid-1770s, just as the American Revolution was heating up. When war broke out in 1775, he hurried to Cambridge, where George Washington had just taken up command of the Continental army. As a gentleman in a largely ragtag army, Burr hoped to attract the notice of Washington, who never warmed to him the way he would Hamilton, whom he met the following year and appointed his chief of staff. Commissioned as a captain, Burr instead attached himself to General Richard Montgomery, who teamed up with (future traitor) Colonel Benedict

Mindful: Young Aaron Burr. Smart, sociable and hard to read, he excelled at Princeton before joining Washington's Continental army. *Wikimedia Commons.*

Arnold for a two-pronged attack on Quebec in December 1775. It was a long-shot effort, and it failed. But Burr distinguished himself in battle, hauling away the body of the felled General Montgomery amid a hail of bullets. Burr was then offered a position on the staff of Washington, but for reasons that are a little mysterious, their relationship never gelled, and Burr found his way to the staff of General Israel Putnam, where he saw combat during the New York campaign of 1776. The following year, he was promoted to lieutenant colonel, where he was often involved in operations in the contested borderlands of greater New York and northern New Jersey and spent the brutal winter of 1777–78 at Valley Forge, where Washington struggled to keep the Continental army together. Washington succeeded and followed it up with the critical Battle of Monmouth in June 1778 (see chapter 3). Burr was at that battle and suffered a heatstroke that led him to seek retirement. Washington instead gave him a furlough and sent him to West Point, after which Burr was assigned to provide order in highly contested Westchester County, New York—a real no-man's land in the American Revolution. Burr performed his duties diligently but found the work exhausting and finally succeeded in receiving his discharge from the army in 1779. Even more than physical exertion was Burr's disgust with army politics.[60]

There was something a bit odd about Burr. He had confidence in spades, and that might be what put Washington off (though no one could call Alexander Hamilton modest). Burr was also a deeply secretive person in his private life, writing many of his letters in cipher. He was known from an early age as a lady's man in what in many ways was a hypersexual age and flirted with poaching the fiancée of John Hancock. (Burr did introduce Madison to Dolley Todd, whom Madison married; Dolley Madison would become one of the most distinguished first ladies in American history).[61]

An air of intrigue and impropriety also surrounded his affair with the woman who became Burr's wife. Theodosia Prevost of Paramus was married to a British officer when Burr met her, probably somewhere in Bergen County in 1777. Prevost's husband was stationed in the southern theater of the war; as a woman of high status, she was treated with civility by rebels and British forces at the Hermitage, the estate where she hosted both. She was about ten years older than Burr and had five children, making her seem like an unlikely choice for a man whose previous paramours included a fourteen-year-old girl. But for all his evident interest in casual sex, Burr was, in the anachronistic terminology of biographer Nancy Isenberg, a "feminist" who gave more credence to women's capacities than most of his peers and was a passionate of fan of Mary Wollstonecraft's 1792 book *A Vindication of the Rights of Women*. Burr's affair with Prevost attracted much gossip, but when her husband conveniently died of illness in Jamaica, the road was open for Burr to marry her, which he did in 1782. In addition to Theodosia's other children, the couple had another surviving daughter, also named Theodosia, on whom Burr doted and emotionally depended on following the elder Theodosia's untimely death in 1794.[62]

After leaving the army, Burr returned to his legal studies and began work as a lawyer in Albany in the closing years of the Revolution. After the British finally evacuated New York City in 1783, he relocated his family to Manhattan—as did Alexander Hamilton, another transplant from Albany to Manhattan with whom Burr began what Hamilton biographer Ron Chernow describes as "a good-natured legal rivalry." They sometimes worked on the same team and others on opposing sides, suspending any disagreement they may have had upon entering dinner parties, where they mingled cordially.[63]

It was a time of unusual opportunity—and a time of new political divisions. The ending of the Revolution had resulted in the flight of Tories and the confiscation of estates; the very fact that Burr and Hamilton were admitted to the bar was the result of relaxed rules amid a shuffling of the social order.[64] Both men were recognized as the city's leading legal talents, but their interests tended in different directions. Burr tended to take cases for the money; Hamilton was more avowedly political. Even though he was a revolutionary who benefited from the displacement of Tories, he soon evinced conservative tendencies that sought to protect established precedents and interests. Amid the uncertainties of the nation's political future in the 1780s, he led the fight for the adoption of the U.S. Constitution and a stronger central government. Burr was silent on these questions.

Hamilton's growing political base was centered in New York. The three main factions there were family-based: the Clintons, the Livingstons and the Schuylers. In the famous words of nineteenth-century Burr biographer James Parton, "The Clintons had the *power*, the Livingstons had *numbers*, and the Schuylers had *Hamilton*." (Hamilton was son-in-law of patriarch Philip Schuyler.) "Neither was strong enough to overcome the other two united, and any two united could overcome the third."[65]

Into this volatile mix entered Burr, who at different points in the years to come would align himself in any number of permutations. George Clinton, who would serve a total of seven terms as governor of New York, appointed him as the state's attorney general in 1789. His entry into electoral politics was of a David defeating Goliath sort: in 1791 he beat Philip Schuyler for a seat in the U.S. Senate. From this point on, his rivalry with Hamilton would intensify in a relationship that can perhaps best be described as frenemies. But Hamilton, who served as President Washington's secretary of the treasury, was a shooting star and one of the most influential figures in American government. His only real rival was Secretary of State Thomas Jefferson.

It was in these years that American politics began evolving toward something the Founding Fathers never expected: a modern party system. They had assumed that men of integrity and intelligence would address the nation's challenges in a disinterested manner, not recognizing that men of integrity and intelligence could have principled disagreements about how to proceed. (The Founders *did* anticipate the reality that there would be men *lacking* intelligence and integrity and crafted a Constitution that did about as well as could be expected to prevent them from overthrowing it.) New York politics at the turn of the nineteenth century continued to be faction-driven but gradually sharpened into two political ideologies: the avowedly elitist, strong-government Federalists and the more egalitarian, decentralization-minded Democratic-Republicans (or Republicans for short). The national leader of the former was Hamilton, that of the latter, Jefferson.

And where was Burr? It was never entirely clear. But over time, there was a hazy drift toward the Republicans. In this there was a bit of a paradox: Hamilton was a man of humble origins who championed a ruling class, while Burr (like Jefferson) was an aristocrat with a democratic accent. Chernow describes Burr as having "a certain patrician hauteur,"[66] even as he forged ties to Jefferson through his old college classmate, James Madison. But what Burr was *really* good at was not so much theorizing but the nuts and bolts of retail politics. A careful listener—and even more careful speaker—he cultivated an unusually devoted coterie of young followers known as "Burrites" and mastered the mechanics of the electoral process.

Burr did this at a time when New York was the ultimate swing state in national politics: New England was solidly Federalist, the South was solidly Republican and the Middle Atlantic states were up for grabs. Madison and Jefferson began courting Burr as an ally in the early 1790s, when Burr was a senator. After finishing his term, Burr did a counterintuitive thing: he took a step down and became a New York state assemblyman. He used the post as a staging ground for the upcoming presidential election of 1800, when incumbent President John Adams would be facing a challenge from Jefferson. He was also deeply involved in land speculation and organized the creation of what was known as the Manhattan Water Company, a utility that was in fact a front for a Republican bank to counter the financial power of Hamilton's Bank of New York. (Shrewdly, he brought in credulous Federalists, including Hamilton's brother-in-law, John Barker Church, on the scheme. The two had a duel in Hoboken after Church accused Burr of bribery; shots were fired but the dispute was resolved when Church apologized.)[67]

Burr's motives could be mysterious, but his ambition was not. In 1796, he jockeyed for electoral votes to become vice president. That gambit didn't work, but he tried again in the following campaign; this time the Jeffersonians were eager to back him as a way of siphoning votes from Adams. Their plan succeeded a little too well: Adams was knocked down to third place—but Burr and Jefferson tied in the Electoral College. Under the prevailing rules, the person who finished first would become president, and the second-place finisher would be vice president. (This would change with the Twelfth Amendment to the Constitution, which specifies designated candidates for the two posts rather than a first-place/second-place finish.) Now, suddenly, it was possible that Burr could take the presidency.

Under the rules of the Constitution, which still apply, a candidate must win an electoral college majority, and in the absence of one, each state delegation in the House of Representatives gets one vote. In 1800, an electoral majority was nine states; in repeated votes, the outcome was Jefferson eight, Burr six (all the New England states, plus Delaware—New Jersey went for Jefferson after having initially going for Adams, as it had in 1796). Burr was gleefully backed by Federalists seeking revenge against the hated Jefferson.

Again the question: And where was Burr in all this? It's not entirely clear. Everybody—Burr included—went into this thinking of him as a vice presidential candidate, something he affirmed shortly after Election Day, when vote tallies were still uncertain. But when asked in late December 1800 whether he would resign the post if actually awarded the presidency, Burr replied that the question was "unnecessary, unreasonable, and impertinent." His implication was that he had already made this clear. On the other hand, Burr never explicitly denied he would take the presidency if he won in the Electoral College.[68]

Ironically, one key figure in this was Burr's rival Hamilton. By 1800, Hamilton had tumbled from the heights of his power a decade earlier. His feuding with Jefferson had led both to resign from Washington's cabinet after his first term, and though he continued to be an influential figure in Federalist politics for the rest of the decade, Hamilton became a more volatile figure, especially after Washington's death in 1799. (His pamphlet attacking fellow Federalist Adams shocked even many of his supporters.) There is no question that Hamilton loathed Jefferson. But by 1800, he loathed Burr even more. "I trust that the Federalists will not finally be so mad as to vote for the latter," he wrote an ally in late December 1800. "I speak with intimate and accurate knowledge of character. His elevation can only promote the purposes of the desperate and the profligate. If there be a man in the world I ought to hate it is Jefferson. With *Burr* I have always been personally well. But the public good must be paramount to every private consideration."[69] The exact sequence of events to follow is shrouded in backroom dealing, but ultimately a switch in the Delaware delegation gave Jefferson the majority. Burr took the oath of office of vice president in March 1801.

He seemed to think things would proceed normally from there. But even if one assumes most Republicans were willing to trust Burr after what had happened, Thomas Jefferson could also be hard to fathom. He was the kind of person who would be openly friendly while privately critical, and despite a civil relationship with Burr, it became increasingly clear that it was Madison—a fellow Virginian—whom Jefferson was grooming as his successor. Burr was largely frozen out of the Jefferson administration even before Jefferson's reelection campaign of 1804, in which he was replaced by George Clinton (a safe sixty-five years old and no long-term threat to Madison in 1808) to nail down the New York vote. Burr turned his attention back to New York and ran for governor that spring of 1804. Hamilton aided and abetted the most crushing electoral defeat in New York history to that point.[70]

Now both men's careers were in eclipse, though comebacks in some form were not out of the question. But a fateful dinner party in Albany in February

1804 altered the trajectory of their lives. Hamilton, assuming he was among friends, spoke freely and critically of Burr, calling him "dangerous." An attendee of the dinner reported this to a friend, who in turn passed this along to a local paper. It was when that attendee wrote that "I could detail a more despicable opinion which Mr. Hamilton expressed to Mr. Burr" that a tipping point was reached. But this fuse burned slowly: the February comments (made amid the gubernatorial election) were reported in April, with Burr hearing of them belatedly and responding in June.[71]

Political invective was a fact of life in the early republic, and Burr, whatever his faults, was never known to be an especially vindictive or prickly person. Hamilton also seemed willing to suspend a grudge: according to Hamilton's brother-in-law Church, Hamilton had actually loaned money to a financially desperate Burr that winter.[72] But whether it was the word *despicable*—a term freighted with connotations of degraded personal behavior[73]—or the culmination of their long-simmering hatred, Burr decided he had enough and demanded an explanation. Hamilton tried to prevaricate without actually apologizing, which Burr regarded as insufficient and challenged him to a duel. Hamilton, who had recently lost his son Philip in a duel, fatalistically agreed. The two men actually socialized, however cooly, at a dinner party at the famed Fraunces Tavern in lower Manhattan a week before the encounter.[74]

Dueling had long been a part of Anglo-American culture, though it was in eclipse in much of the United States by 1800—indeed, it was illegal in both New York and New Jersey, though it continued to be practiced in the South for decades to come (Andrew Jackson famously carried a bullet in his body for decades after one of his). Dueling was regarded as a way for men to defend their honor—"elaborate forms of conflict resolution," as Ron Chernow explained, "which is why duelists did not automatically try and kill their opponents."[75] Duels were facilitated by "seconds" chosen by each side who conducted negotiations as to how, when and where duels would happen. In the case of Burr and Hamilton, this would be pistols, on July 11, in Weehawken.

Weehawken sits on the New Jersey Palisades, about two hundred feet above the Hudson River. From the New York side, it appeared to be a straight drop to the water, but at low tide there was a small beach covered with vegetation that could be cleared as needed. By 7:00 a.m. on that fateful July day, the dueling parties had assembled to attend to their grim business.[76]

As with so much else in Burr's life, much of what followed is uncertain and contested. In a statement he wrote before the duel, Hamilton expressed his opposition to dueling, stating that "I am conscious of no ill-will to Col. Burr, distinct from political opposition, which, as I trust, has proceeded from pure and upright motives," and indicated that he intended to throw his first shot away (under the rules, he would have two). But whether in fact Hamilton's errant shot was indeed thrown away is contested, and there is evidence, like his decision to put on his spectacles, that indicated he cared about his aim. Burr biographer Nancy Isenberg contends that Hamilton used his final testament to present "an idealized version of himself, while making use of one last opportunity to blacken Burr's name."[77]

Burr's state of mind at the time seemed more pragmatic. His correspondence on the eve of the duel focused more on his financial affairs (which were dreadful), and he placed his private correspondence in the care of his daughter (it would later be lost in a shipwreck). He seemed far less conflicted about the task at hand. When given the cue to fire, he did not

Not Throwing Away His Shot: Climactic moment of the Burr-Hamilton showdown, July 11, 1804. *Library of Congress.*

throw away his shot and hit Hamilton in the abdomen. "I am a dead man," Hamilton said, though he survived long enough to get back across the river and die surrounded by family, who hadn't known he'd gone to Weehawken for a duel.[78]

Hamilton's death was greeted with shock and grief. It was also greeted with outrage: Burr was indicted for murder in New Jersey. (He was also indicted in New York, which is a bit odd, because the duel took place outside state jurisdiction, and no one had ever been prosecuted for it before.)[79] Burr did have supporters in New Jersey, among them his old friend and Federalist Jonathan Dayton. Friends in Congress wrote a letter to the state's governor, Joseph Bloomfield, asking him to nullify the indictment, but the effort failed. Burr also relied on Aaron Ogden, part of a storied Jersey dynasty, to represent him in court cases.[80]

Still, as with the aftermath of his actions in the election of 1800, Burr seemed to think he could resume something like his old life. This did not appear likely. On the other hand, many observers, especially in the South and West, did not see anything problematic in what had happened, and may well have thought Hamilton deserved what he got. Burr was still vice president for about another seven months, and he returned to Washington, where he presided over the trial of Samuel Chase, a Supreme Court justice Jefferson was trying to expel from office. (Chase was acquitted.) Jefferson even invited Burr to several dinner parties.[81]

But appearances were deceiving. Once Jefferson's second term began, Burr was, in effect, a man without a country. And he began to think of himself literally that way. This is undoubtedly why he became involved in a shadowy and complex plot that involved land sales, private armies, the annexation of Spanish territory in the Southwest—and, allegedly, a plot of secession from the United States. Burr was caught and brought to Washington and underwent two separate trials for treason. In both cases, the evidence was circumstantial and he was acquitted. Now a nomad, he went abroad—to England, Sweden and France, among other countries— alternately regarded with curiosity and courteousness as well as dismay and contempt. He eventually returned to New York, resumed work as a lawyer and was involved in a late-life divorce scandal with an elderly widow. Burr died in September 1836, a few months after James Madison, making him the longest lived of the Founders. He was buried in Princeton, adjacent to his grandfather Reverend Edwards.

At the start and at the finish—and much of the time in between—Aaron Burr was, for better and worse, a son of New Jersey.

IN THE CENTURIES AFTER his death, Burr has had his champions. The famed nineteenth-century biographer James Parton was one. Gore Vidal, a novelist who wrote a series of iconoclastic fictionalized histories, was another, in his intriguing 1973 installment *Burr*. (He suggested that what enraged Burr was Hamilton's insinuation of him of having an incestuous relationship with his beloved daughter Theodosia.) In her 2007 biography *Fallen Founder*, Nancy Isenberg noted that many of the charges leveled at Burr—womanizing, unethical business practices, political intrigue, enslaving African Americans—could be leveled at Hamilton or Jefferson with the same force. Even many of his filibustering activities were not regarded as illegal (Jackson, an admirer, would take them a good deal further in his activities in Florida in the 1810s). A persuasive condemnation of Burr best rests on a preponderance of evidence rather than a smoking gun.

The most intriguing recent assessment of Burr came from Lin-Manuel Miranda in his 2015 musical *Hamilton*. As its very title implies, Burr is the

MONUMENTAL: Memorial to Alexander Hamilton in Hamilton Park, Weehawken. The city he helped make great is on the other side of the Hudson River. *Jim Cullen*.

antagonist—but a complex, even impressive, one. And a deeply human one: one of the most moving songs in the show is "Dear Theodosia," in which the characters of Burr and Hamilton harmonize in expressing their love for their respective children.

American history will never be simple or boring as long as Aaron Burr figures in the story.

5

MISS BARTON FOUNDS A SCHOOL IN BORDENTOWN

A TALENTED ADMINISTRATOR NURSES AMBITIONS THAT TAKE HER IN UNEXPECTED DIRECTIONS

There are some people who seem to know what they want to do with their lives pretty much from the outset. Sometimes that knowledge is relatively general, like "I want to work with my hands." Or it's relatively specific, like "I want to be an actor." And sometimes, that's what happens. But often it doesn't, whether because the competition is too great, interests change, or intervening events redirect the course of one's life. Still, more often than not, character shapes destiny: when you have a choice in the matter, the work you do reflects your background and personality.

It seemed pretty clear what Clara Barton was destined to be: a teacher. She came from a family of teachers, showed early talent for teaching and compiled an impressive track record of success (though one that revealed a certain restlessness of spirit). It was this sense of ambition that brought her to western New Jersey, where Barton quickly established herself as a force to be reckoned with—"a quiet will," to quote the title of a biography written by a distant relative—in establishing New Jersey's first public school.[82] And then Barton encountered a powerful force that has blocked individual aspiration and social progress in many lives: sexism. She could not single-handedly defeat it. But she also refused to accept it. Ultimately, the choices Barton made in dealing with the limitations imposed on her as a woman were important not simply in her own life, or as a role model for others, but in transforming that most typically masculine of human experiences: warfare. Barton improved education in New Jersey to the best of her ability. And then she improved health care in the nation—and the world at large.

Like Jonathan Edwards (chapter 2) a century earlier, Clara Barton was a quintessential Yankee—a fact that would play an important role in shaping her identity. Her ancestor Edward Barton emigrated from England to Salem, Massachusetts, circa 1640, and eventually settled in Maine, then part of the Massachusetts Bay Colony. Her family later migrated down to North Oxford, where her father, Captain Stephen Barton (1774–1862), fought Indians on the northwestern frontier of Ohio and Michigan under the famed Revolutionary War general Anthony Wayne.

Barton's maternal history is also important. Her great-aunt was Martha Moore Ballard (1735–1812), a once-obscure Maine midwife immortalized by the great Harvard historian Laurel Thatcher Ulrich in her Pulitzer Prize–winning book *A Midwife's Tale*.[83] This genealogy may help explain Barton's subsequent fate in the medical profession.

Barton herself was born as Clarissa Harlowe Barton on Christmas Day 1821, the youngest (by a decade) of five children. Her name reflects yet another legacy: a literary one. Samuel Richardson's 1748 novel *Clarissa Harlowe* is one of the foundational works of English literature, the story of a young woman who struggles to preserve her honor amid family pressure. The child was quickly nicknamed Clara, a moniker she retained for life.[84]

Barton soon evinced talents worthy of her pedigree. She was able to read by age three; she began school at age four. Both of her sisters and eldest brother were teachers (though her oldest sister suffered from severe mental illness).[85] The portrait that emerges of Barton's childhood is a complex one. On the one hand, she was an excellent equestrienne who could hit a bull's-eye with a revolver from fifty feet away, able to wield a hammer and drive a wagon team—her father described her as "more boy than girl." On the other hand, she was quite shy, and while she was home-schooled when young, her parents briefly sent her to a local boarding school hoping it would overcome her timidity. There is also a glimpse of her future career when the ten-year-old Barton nursed her older brother David through a sustained illness.[86]

WARM REGARD: Clara Barton, circa 1850. Barton founded the first public school in New Jersey. But the outcome was unhappy for her. *Wikimedia Commons.*

By the time of her adolescence, Barton had conquered her shyness and had received an excellent education. She passed a teaching exam in 1839, when she was seventeen years old. By then Barton had launched a career that that brought her to a series of schools in central Massachusetts, where she was in high demand. She wielded her authority lightly but could crack down when needed. When working one morning at a challenging school, she found herself dealing with an arrogantly tardy student. She asked him to come to the front of the room, and when he swaggered forward, Barton pulled a riding whip out of her desk, wielding it to trip him as the rest of the class looked on in horror. She then dismissed students for the day, suggesting a picnic in a meadow near the school. "None ever need more than a kindly smile," she subsequently reported.[87]

Barton also demonstrated tough-mindedness when dealing with her superiors. When asked to teach a winter term at a particularly challenging school where women were paid at a summer rate rather than a full salary, she refused: "I may sometimes be willing to teach for nothing, but if paid at all, I shall never do a man's work for less than a man's pay." The school board acquiesced to her demands and went on to give her further assignments.[88]

In 1851, Barton decided it was time to make a change and enrolled in the Clinton Liberal Institute in Clinton, New York. Established by the Universalist Church (of which she was lifelong, if nominal, member), the institute provided her with intellectual stimulation that was augmented by nearby Hamilton College. She took courses in languages, math, science, philosophy and religion.[89] Barton also became romantically involved with the principal of the school but never married him or anyone else. As a nephew to whom she confided later explained, "She could think of herself as with satisfaction as a wife or mother, but that on the whole she felt she had been more useful to the world by being free of matrimonial ties."[90]

After a return visit home, the next stop on Barton's journey was New Jersey, where she went to visit friends from the Clinton Institute in Hightstown. While there, she was unexpectedly offered a teaching job in nearby Cedarville, though she was troubled that the school where she worked was funded by subscription (in other words, tuition). After finishing a term there, she left for Bordentown, a village about a dozen miles away that attracted her attention during a visit in 1852. Founded in the late seventeenth century, Bordentown was a thriving community on the Delaware River. It got pretty thoroughly worked over during the Revolution—occupied by the British, much of it burned down—but had sprung back by the time Barton arrived (and its historical district maintains much of its nineteenth-century charm to this day, with many of its buildings registered as state and national sites).

Soon after her arrival, Barton became concerned about the situation of boys in Bordentown. At the time, there were no public schools in New Jersey—indeed, the notion of taxpayer-funded education was largely limited to New England. The reform-minded Barton traveled to the nearby state

ELEMENTARY: Clara Barton School on Crosswicks Street. Note marker tracing the town's seventeenth-century history. Bordentown was a thriving village when Barton was there. *Jim Cullen.*

capital of Trenton in a bid to convince lawmakers of the need for public schools. But she got nowhere.[91]

Barton was not ready to give up on the idea, however. She continued to grapple with the problem of lost boys in the streets of the town.

> *I found them on all sides of me. Every street corner had little knots of them, idle, listless as if to say, what shall one do, when one has nothing to do? I sought every inconspicuous occasion to stop and talk with them. I saw nothing unusual in them. Much like other boys I had known, unusually courteous, showing special instruction in that line, and frequently of unusual intelligence. They spoke of their banishment from school with far less of boasting than would have been expected, and often with regret. "Lady, there is no school for us," answered a bright-faced lad of fourteen, as he rested his foot on the edge of a little park fountain where I accosted him. "We would be glad to go if there was one."[92]*

Barton changed tactics. She approached the local postmaster, who was also the chairman of Bordentown's School Committee, and floated the idea of starting a local taxpayer-funded institution. The postmaster was sympathetic but skeptical. "These boys were renegades, many of them more fit for the penitentiary—a woman could do nothing with them," he told her. "They wouldn't go to school if they had the chance, and the parents would never send them to a 'pauper school.'" The town would turn on her if she tried.[93]

Undeterred, Barton persisted with a specific proposal: if the town would pay for a building and supply it, she would teach for free. The chairman continued to be skeptical, acknowledging the generosity of Barton's offer but indicating that it was ill-timed and impractical. Barton responded politely but forcefully:

> *With all respect for the prejudices of the people, I should try not to increase them. My only desire was to open and teach a school in Bordentown, to which its outcast children could go and be taught; and I would emphasize that desire by adding that I wished no salary. I would open and teach such a school, without remuneration, but my effort must have the majesty of the law, and the power vested in its offices behind it or it could not stand....In fact, it must stand as by their order, leaving the work and results to me.[94]*

Barton's proposal was notable for its idealism and shrewdness: She was demonstrating altruism and driving a hard bargain at the same time. "I was not there for necessity. I needed nothing of them," she later explained (though one wonders, given her less than cushy personal circumstances, how long she could hold out without a salary). Barton was demanding power: the right to work as she saw fit, with institutional backing both in the form of financing as well as administrative authority. She was well on her way to becoming the skilled bureaucratic in-fighter she would remain for the rest of her life.

The postmaster/chair asked Barton if he could bring her proposal to the full school board. She was surprised to be invited to meet with it the next day, whereupon the board approved her plan unanimously. A 1798 schoolhouse was retrofitted along the lines she requested—she insisted on and got blackboards—and opened in July 1852.[95]

Barton's enterprise got off to a fast start. On opening day, she had six students; the next day she had twenty and the day after that forty. Originally, the school was designated for boys, but she took on girls, too. Demand was so great that Bordentown opened a second school over a tailor's shop, and Barton recruited a friend from North Oxford to run

Educating: The Clara Barton Schoolhouse, founded in 1852. It was rededicated in honor of Barton's two hundredth birthday in 2021. *Wikimedia Commons.*

it. By this point, there were four hundred children hoping to enroll, and the town made plans to build a new facility to house the school-age population of six hundred.[96]

Barton was not only an able administrator but also showed real talent as a teacher. Part of the early success of the school was her decision in the early days for students and teacher to get to know one another. Barton was also open to the world around her. She had her advanced students read Harriet Beecher Stowe's huge antislavery bestseller *Uncle Tom's Cabin*, for example—the *Star Wars* or *Harry Potter* of its time, but with a political twist. When teaching U.S. history and the nation's origins in self-government, she asked students to design their own code of conduct. The school board was alarmed by this, but Barton sought and received time for a trial run. "You must either remain as you are or redeem yourselves," she told the students. They rose to the occasion. By the school's second year of operation, Barton was receiving a $250 annual salary—about the going rate for a professional educator, most of whom were women. Barton's idea also caught on more broadly: by 1855, twenty-nine towns in New Jersey had opened public schools.[97]

Bordentown's gleaming new public school was completed in 1853 to great hopes. Made of plastered brick, it was two stories high, contained eight classrooms and was supplied with new desks, maps, and other equipment. Students were graded by age, reflecting the growing specialization and sophistication of American education. Schoolhouse Number 1, as it was dubbed, opened that fall with great fanfare.[98]

That said, the success of public schooling in Bordentown was creating structural frictions that would soon engulf Barton. Now that taxpayers were willing to support education, religious groups came forward demanding a share of funds for their institutions. The opening of free schools threatened the business model of private schools funded by subscription. The town tried to find places for these teachers in the public school, but the upheavals bred resentment.[99]

But Barton's biggest problem was gender bias. Deciding that a woman could not handle the responsibility of running the new public school, the board appointed a man at a salary of $500 a year, leaving Barton and her colleague with a title of "female assistant" at the old salary of $250. They tried to swallow their pride but inevitably chafed as they saw the school go in directions they didn't like. In February 1854, both quit in frustration. The *Bordentown Register* criticized them for "forsaking their posts without leave or warning."[100]

Bordentown was the crossroads of Barton's career. By this point, it was already clear that she was principled, skillful and resilient in the face of opposition. And when faced with a situation she found unacceptable, she had the courage to walk away. But the stand she took had a price, and it wasn't only, or even primarily, financial. She suffered a physical as well as emotional breakdown.

Barton pivoted, literally and figuratively. Her family urged her to return home, but she felt it would be a step backward. In the winter of 1854, she relocated to Washington, D.C., and landed a job as a copyist in the U.S. Patent Office. Nevertheless, she wasn't yet ready to give up what she regarded as her vocation. "She continued to think of herself as a teacher," a biographer noted. "The schoolroom had become temporarily impractical, and she wanted to come to Washington and spend time enough in the capital of the Nation to know something about it." It is ironic, then, that the District of Columbia would be the focal point for the rest of her life.[101]

Barton performed notably well at the Patent Office—the handwriting skills she had cultivated as a classroom teacher came in handy—and was soon promoted to the position of clerk, which paid the princely sum of $1,400 annually. Not surprisingly, the appointment generated resentment among her male colleagues, who harassed her and tried to get her dismissed. But she had a boss who stood by her over the course of the next three years.[102]

Then Barton also ran into a different kind of politics—the presidential kind. She had been appointed to her position under the umbrella of the administration of Franklin Pierce, a Democrat from New Hampshire (which is to say a New Englander; Barton's father had been a Jacksonian Democrat).[103] In 1856, James Buchanan of Pennsylvania was elected president. His new administration purged the federal government of so-called Black Republicans—a term applied broadly to those who supported rights for African Americans. Barton, who had avowedly declared herself sympathetic to the new party (she often visited the halls of Congress and heard speeches there), lost her job.[104] She returned to Massachusetts.

This may well have been the most difficult phase of Barton's life. Teaching still seemed like the most likely choice for a career, as it was one of the few avenues really open to women in the nineteenth century. By this point, however, Barton had left education behind. "I have outgrown that," she told a nephew, noting the low pay. The question was what else she could do, and the answer was far from obvious. By the summer of 1860,

Barton's frustration and anxiety had driven her to a nervous breakdown. She spent two months with friends in upstate New York, haunted by suicidal longings.

Desperate for anything, Barton accepted a job as a temporary copyist in Washington at the end of 1860. She arrived in nation's capital at a time of intense polarization in the aftermath of a presidential election that would bring Abraham Lincoln to the White House the following spring. Though an avowed Yankee, Barton was concerned about the fanaticism she perceived among antislavery activists. "It matters little to them that every rounded sentence that falls from their chiseled lips, every burst of eloquence which 'brings down the house,' drive home one more rivet in slavery's chain," she noted. "Men talk flippantly of dissolving the Union. This may happen, but in my humble opinion never till our very horses gallop in blood." Barton heard, and liked, Lincoln's inaugural address, which showed both firmness in maintaining the Union even as he struck a conciliatory tone toward seceding Southerners.[105]

As it turned out, it was seceding Southerners who struck first blood—and prompted Barton to respond in a way that changed her life. The official outbreak of the Civil War occurred on April 12, 1861, when the newly formed Confederates States of America fired on Fort Sumter off the coast of Charleston, South Carolina. The Union commander surrendered, and there were no casualties. But a week later on April 19—Barton noted it as the eighty-sixth anniversary of the outbreak of the American Revolution—an angry mob in Baltimore attached the Massachusetts Sixth Regiment, which was marching from Boston to Washington to protect the capital. Twelve civilians and four soldiers were killed in the violence, and the battered troops, a number of them wounded, boarded trains to take them the rest of the way.[106]

When Barton heard about the incident, she rushed to the train station. She knew some of the men of the Massachusetts Sixth—they had been "schoolmates and playmates" from back home. She led several women who were also at the station to dress the injuries of the wounded with handkerchiefs. When the Sixth was moved to the U.S. Senate Chamber because there were no barracks available to them, Barton visited and assessed the situation. She quickly organized an effort to supply the regiment with food and supplies.[107] The nation was woefully unprepared in medical infrastructure, but that would change rapidly.

If Bordentown was the place where Barton lost her way in 1854, Washington is where she found her life's work in 1861. Using political connections that included Massachusetts U.S. Senator Henry Wilson, Barton soon found her way to the front, where she was on the battlefield for engagements such as Cedar Mountain and the Second Battle of Bull Run in 1862. There were other prominent women who were making a significant contribution to the war effort, among them Dorothea Dix, a reformer who did much work advocating for the mentally ill before the war and who became the superintendent of nurses during the conflict, and Mary Livermore, who played an important role in the U.S. Sanitary Commission. But Barton was unique for the degree to which she placed herself in harm's way. After the Battle of Antietam—the bloodiest day in American history—Barton, who was on-site, got the nickname "angel of the battlefield." It stuck for generations. By war's end she was appointed "lady in charge" of field hospitals for the Army of the James (River) and became an expert in what we now think of as triage: assessing the health of wounded soldiers and what, if anything, could be done for them. Her position at the front also made her a clearinghouse for information, and days before he died, President Lincoln appointed her to a position where she helped families determine the fate of lost soldiers and paroled prisoners.

Clara Barton had found her vocation. In years to come, she was on the scene of the Franco-Prussian War, provided relief during the Paris Commune and founded the American Red Cross. Her activism led her to cross paths with luminaries that included Frederick Douglass, Susan B.

STAMPED: Clara Barton commemorative postage, issued in 1948. After her failed foray in Bordentown, Barton found worldwide fame in nursing. *Wikimedia Commons.*

Anthony and Kaiser Wilhelm of Germany, who awarded her a medal for her labors. In the closing years of the nineteenth century, she focused on natural disasters, among them the notorious Johnstown Flood of 1889, the deadliest catastrophe of its time. And when the Spanish-American War broke out, the seventy-seven-year-old Barton was on the scene in Havana. She made her final mission on behalf of the Red Cross in 1900, when she traveled to Galveston in the aftermath of what is still the deadliest hurricane in American history.[108] She published a memoir of her childhood in 1907 before dying of pneumonia five years later. Few lives were more consequential.

CLARA BARTON DID NOT have an easy life, and she was not always an easy person with whom to work. "There were times when Barton admitted her shortcomings or the disappointments of her life, but they were rare, and never public," her most rigorous biographer has noted. "She was certain of her abilities, yet always unsure whether others shared her high regard." As this writer noted, Barton could be thin-skinned, self-righteous and rebellious, and she suffered frequent bouts of depression.[109] It has never been easy for American women to work outside the home—or, for that matter, inside it—but Barton's lot was more challenging than most. And while she had a number of serious romantic relationships in her life, she never had the comfort of a lifelong companion. This was the price of professional success in her time and place.

Barton's frustration in Bordentown might not have been the most trying moment in her life (though it likely was among them). In any event, it was the most consequential, for her failure to achieve her dream of a career in education set her on a path where she would go on to have a global impact. There are any number of ways in which she may rightly be regarded as an inspiration. Few people in American life have failed so fruitfully.

6

MR. WHITMAN BUYS
A HOME IN CAMDEN

AN "OBSCENE" WRITER SETTLES IN AS A "GOOD GRAY
POET" AT THE TWILIGHT OF HIS CAREER

> *Camerado, this is no book,*
> *Who touches this touches a man,*
> *(Is it night? are we together alone?)*
> *It is I you hold and who holds you*
> *I spring from the pages into your arms—decease calls me forth*
> *—Walt Whitman, "So Long!" (1860–1881)*

In March 1884, sixty-four-year-old Walt Whitman did something he had never done before: he bought a house. It was in the thriving city of Camden, New Jersey. Whitman's purchase was striking for a number of reasons. The first is that he had had led a fairly peripatetic life. Born on Long Island, he moved back and forth between there and Brooklyn in his youth and young adulthood. He spent much of the Civil War and its aftermath in Washington, D.C. Whitman moved around a lot even when he resided in these places—walking the streets of Manhattan, for example, or visiting hospitals around the nation's capital during the war. Such perambulations were in fact central to his artistry, notably his masterwork *Leaves of Grass* (1855–92), a work of poetry stuffed with firsthand observations of what he saw, heard and felt in his everyday interactions with ordinary Americans. Whitman would continue to wander even after he bought that piece of real estate in Camden, though

GOOD GRAY POET: Walt Whitman, 1887. By this point, the native Long Islander had become a longtime Camden resident. *Library of Congress.*

his ambit would narrow, and that house would ultimately become his hospice.

The second striking thing about this transaction is that he could afford it. Whitman had been able to support himself (and contribute to the care of his mentally and physically disabled brother) over the course of his life, but he had never been wealthy—and he never made much money as a writer. But his publishing income began to rise after the Civil War, in part because he was increasingly able to place his work in newspapers and magazines, and also because he began to attract a coterie of admirers, some of them quite wealthy, who were generous with their support. The house he bought cost $1,750, of which $1,250 came from book royalties and the other $500 from newspaper publisher George W. Childs.[110] In the years that followed, Whitman would increasingly be the beneficiary of gifts from his circle of supporters. By the end of his life, he was not wealthy, but he was financially comfortable.

The third striking aspect of Whitman's house is where it was. In popular memory, Whitman is known as a quintessential New Yorker—certainly the city (though Brooklyn and Manhattan were separate municipalities until six years after his death), but also Long Island (his birthplace is maintained as a museum across the street from the mall that bears his name). But Whitman spent the last quarter of his life in New Jersey, initially because of a health emergency but ultimately because he liked it. He became a luminary in his adopted final hometown of Camden, hosting visitors from all over the world in a house that continues to function as a cultural attraction to this day. That house, at 328 Mickle Street (now Martin Luther King Boulevard), is on the National Register of Historical Places, operated by the New Jersey Division of Parks and Forestry.

But if you really want to find him, look under your boot soles—or across the national horizon he made his own.

> *Flow on, river! flow with the flood-tide, and ebb with the ebb-tide!*
> *Frolic on, crested and scallop-edg'd waves!*
> *Gorgeous clouds of the sunset! drench with your splendor me, or the men*
>   *and women generations after me!*
> —*Walt Whitman, "Crossing Brooklyn Ferry" (1860–1881)*

WALT WHITMAN LIVED HIS life, from beginning to end, at waters' edge. He was born in West Hills (now Huntington) Long Island, on May 31, 1819. The town sits on Long Island Sound; in the years to come, Whitman would find himself adjacent to rivers—East, Hudson, Potomac, Delaware—and the Atlantic Ocean until he landed in Camden, where he would frequently take ferries for day trips to Philadelphia.

Whitman was the second of nine children. His father's family was English; his mother's was Dutch, and his birthplace was the borderland between the two colonial empires. Whitman had a great-uncle who died at the Battle of Brooklyn in 1776 and claimed one of his earliest childhood memories was an embrace by the Marquis de Lafayette when the French hero of the American Revolution toured the country in 1824–25.[111] The Whitman family moved to Brooklyn when Walt was four years old, and he attended public schools there. By the time of his early adolescence, the family was back out east, with Whitman doing odd jobs in the printing business that led to a series of jobs for Long Island newspapers. He taught

LITERARY DESTINATION: Exterior of Whitman's house. He entertained a steady stream of visitors, among them famous writers and poets. *Jim Cullen.*

85

school in a series of towns there between 1836 and 1841, when he moved to Manhattan and became a full-time journalist.

The next fourteen years were the crucible of Whitman's career. He edited and wrote for a series of publications (including a short stint for a paper in New Orleans in 1848), crisscrossing between Brooklyn and Manhattan. He also got involved in politics as a generally antislavery Democrat. But Whitman's real work in these years was soaking up the nation and people he loved. He was a passionate fan of opera and theater—pop music in those days— sauntering the streets of the city and observing his fellow citizens at work and play ("Crossing Brooklyn Ferry" was a love song to commuters). In addition to reviews and reporting, Whitman made a foray into fiction; his 1842 novel *Franklin Evans* tells the story of a Long Islander who becomes an alcoholic, a topic that reflected the prominent temperance movement of the time. There was little indication Whitman was on the verge of a major literary career as he quietly built up a body of poems—though with his restless sense of meter and lack of rhyme, many of his peers would not readily regard his poetry as such.

Whitman's technical know-how and media savvy allowed him to self-publish his first book of poems, *Leaves of Grass*, in 1855, a book that would undergo steady expansion and revision in a series of new editions over the course of the next thirty-seven years. (The first edition of *Leaves of Grass* had a dozen poems, the last over three hundred.) Its title is a pun: "leaves" as a synonym for pages as well as humble blades in a field, reflecting his fierce love of democracy. Yet the book is also a celebration of individualism and interpersonal dialogue, as reflected in its famous opening poem "Song of Myself":

> *I celebrate myself, and sing myself,*
> *And what I assume you shall assume,*
> *For every atom belonging to me as good belongs to you.*

Whitman sent of a copy of *Leaves of Grass* to Ralph Waldo Emerson, the preeminent celebrity intellectual of the day. "I find it the most extraordinary piece of wit and wisdom that America has yet contributed," Emerson replied. "I greet you at the beginning of a great career."[112] Emerson later tempered his enthusiasm, in part out of irritation that Whitman published Emerson's letter without permission in the second edition of *Leaves of Grass*. But it was clear to Emerson and anyone else who was paying attention at the time that a strikingly new literary voice—brash, passionate, at times profane—had emerged on the American scene.

The problem is not all that many people *were* paying attention. Whitman printed 795 copies of the first edition of *Leaves of Grass*, which did not sell out. After the second edition of 1856, he followed it up with a third in 1860, this time issued by the respected Boston publishing house of Thayer and Eldridge. This edition actually sold in the low thousands, but such figures were paltry compared with peers such as Nathaniel Hawthorne—not to mention superstars like Charles Dickens or the women writers who dominated the publishing industry of the time, notably Harriet Beecher Stowe, whose 1851 novel *Uncle Tom's Cabin* sold millions.[113]

But Whitman had a bigger problem: his work was widely considered obscene. His poems were notable for their graphic sexuality—heterosexual, homosexual (though this was not widely discussed or recognized as such at the time) and masturbatory. This is evident as even this brief (and relatively mild) passage from "Song of Myself" suggests:

> *I mind how once we lay such a transparent summer morning,*
> *How you settled your head athwart my hips and gently turn'd over upon me,*
> *And parted the shirt from my bosom-bone, and plunged your tongue to my*
> *   bare-stript heart,*
> *And reach'd till you felt my beard, and reach'd till you held my feet.*

"It is impossible to imagine how any man's fancy could have conceived such a mass of stupid filth, unless he were possessed of the soul of a sentimental donkey that had died of disappointed love," wrote the renowned critic Rufus Griswold in an 1855 review of *Leaves of Grass*. "This *poet* (?) without wit, but with a certain vagrant wildness, just serves to show the energy which natural imbecility is occasionally capable of under strong excitement."[114] Such views would define respectable opinion about *Leaves of Grass* for many years to come.

Whitman continued writing poetry and prose, but he was also deeply immersed in the cataclysmic event of his time: the Civil War. He was a passionate supporter of Abraham Lincoln—subject of some of his most memorable poems—and the Union cause. He did not join in the army (at forty-one, he was not prime fighting age), but his brother George, ten years his junior, enlisted and fought in a series of battles. When Whitman read a report of a soldier with a similar name who had been injured, fearing it was George, he ventured to Virginia and witnessed the war's devastation firsthand. (George was later captured and freed in the final months of the war.) Whitman spent the latter years of the conflict regularly visiting hospitals in the nation's capital, offering small gifts and good cheer to the wounded. He managed to pick up some odd government jobs to support himself. In January 1865, he was appointed to a more solid position at the Bureau of Indian Affairs and published a book of poems, *Drum Taps* (it would later be incorporated into *Leaves of Grass*). But he was fired from the position because his boss, Secretary of Interior James Harlan, considered Whitman's work indecent. "I will not have the author of that book in this department," Harlan stated. "No, even if the President of the United States should order his reinstatement, I would resign sooner than I would have him back."[115] An ally arranged for Whitman's transfer to the Attorney General's Office, where he spent the next seven years. Another ally in the Interior Department, Douglas O'Connor, who was also an editor at the *Saturday Evening Post*, wrote an admiring 1866 biography of Whitman, *The Good Gray Poet*, which marked a turning point in his reputation, further enhanced by a fourth edition of *Leaves of Grass* in 1867, which contained his most famous poem, "Oh Captain! My Captain," a tribute to Lincoln that was uncharacteristic in Whitman's body of work because it rhymed. In 1871, Whitman published a fifth edition of *Leaves of Grass*, along with two other books: *Democratic Vistas*, a volume of political commentary, and the long poem *A Passage to India*. It looked like he had attained a measure of security as a civil servant, even as his literary reputation took root.

And then disaster struck—changing the course of his life and also his location.

> *The touch of flame—the illuminating fire—the loftiest look at last,*
> *O'er city, passion, sea—o'er prairie mountain, wood, the earth itself;*
> *The airy, different, changing hues of all, in falling twilight....*
> —*Walt Whitman, "Old Age's Lambent Peaks" (1888–89)*

January 23, 1873, was a miserable day in Washington—raw with rain and sleet—and Whitman spent it in his office at the Treasury Department. He stayed late and picked up a novel by Edward Bulwer-Lytton, a bestselling writer of the time, which he read while lying on a sofa before a fire. He felt dizzy but decided to go home, declining an offer by a concerned guard to walk him home. Whitman woke up in the middle of the night without sensation or able to move his left side. He had suffered a stroke.[116]

Whitman recovered slowly. He lingered for a few months in Washington, but that May he went down to visit mother, Louisa, who was living with his brother George in Camden, New Jersey. In the years after the Civil War, George Whitman had prospered in the building business. He got a job as a pipe inspector in Camden, shuttling between there and another job in Brooklyn until his marriage in 1871, at which point he settled down in New Jersey. George and his wife (also named Louisa) bought a house at 322 Stevens Street in the city, and his mother and disabled brother Eddie soon came to live with the newlyweds. Walt's trip was prompted by his mother's final decline, and he arrived a few days before her death.[117]

Whitman returned to Washington for a few weeks but felt broken in body and spirit. He accepted an offer from George and Louisa to come to Camden and took a leave of absence from his job that proved to be permanent. He would live in the couple's household on Stevens Street for the next eleven years, providing him with support and comfort in a difficult stretch that included a second stroke in 1875 that affected the right side of his body. Fortunately, it was not as serious as the first.

Camden in the 1870s was a burgeoning industrial city, one reminiscent of the Brooklyn of Whitman's youth. Originally a Dutch settlement, the town was named after British statesman Charles Pratt, Earl of Camden, who had sided with the colonists during the American Revolution.

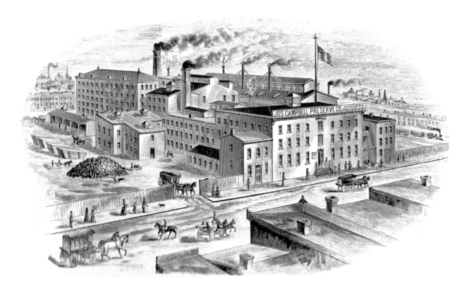

INDUSTRIOUS: An 1894 etching of Camden when Whitman lived there. Note the prominence of the Campbell Soup Company, a longtime fixture of the city. *Wikimedia Commons*.

Incorporated as a city in 1828, Camden grew rapidly thanks to its strategic location just across the Delaware River from Philadelphia. Indeed, one could say that as New York was to Brooklyn, Philadelphia was to Camden—no doubt part of its psychic appeal to Whitman. The city was a major manufacturing center (Campbell Soup Company, founded in 1869, remains headquartered there to this day) and a major rail link between New York, Philadelphia and Atlantic City. The rumble of trains was a feature of Whitman's everyday life there that he quite enjoyed as a symbol of high-tech modernity in a nation that was growing by leaps and bounds. "I sit and watch them long—& think of you," he wrote of the trains to Eddie Doyle, a transit worker who had been Whitman's longtime companion when he lived in Washington.[118]

By the late 1870s, Whitman had shaken off his physical and mental maladies and resumed his literary career, which he sustained by working out of his room on Stevens Street. In 1881, he published his fifth edition of *Leaves of Grass*, the last in which he made significant changes in terms of adding new poems and rearranging old ones like "So Long!" (See epigraph of this chapter.) He signed a contract with the Osgood publishing company of Boston, which put him in the big leagues, as that was the house of renowned authors such as William Dean Howells and Mark Twain. But in 1882 the district attorney of Boston declared the book indecent and demanded it be withdrawn—for a long time afterward, the phrase "Banned in Boston" became a badge of honor for free speech advocates decrying the Puritan prudery of that city—and Whitman pivoted by having the book issued by the Philadelphia house of Rees Welsh. This was the most commercially successful edition of Whitman's lifetime, selling thousands of copies. He was also earning royalties from British editions of his work as well as payment for his newspaper writing.[119]

Though at the time and since there was a narrative, some of it stoked by Whitman himself, that he was being consigned to undeserved obscurity, his fame was growing in these years. In 1880, the well-known poet, essayist and critic Edmund Clarence Stedman wrote an appraisal of Whitman for the highbrow *Scribner's* magazine that captured his reputation in his Camden years. "Let us be candid: no writer holds, in some respects, a more enviable place than Walt Whitman," Stedman noted. But "curiously enough, three-fourths of the articles upon Mr. Whitman assert that he is totally neglected by the press."[120]

Whitman was also recovering physically. While his house with his brother and sister-in-law Camden remained his base, he was out of town for twenty-six weeks in 1877, twenty-eight in 1879 and twenty-four in 1881. Whitman traveled as far as Denver and Canada in these years and also enjoyed making treks to nearby Timber Creek, where he hoped to build a summer cottage. Whitman also delivered a series of lectures on Abraham Lincoln around the Northeast, for which he was well paid. Because he had little in the way of overhead, he could save money.[121]

This, then, was the context for Whitman's declaration of dependence from George and Louisa in 1884 (Eddie had been moved to an asylum by then). When couple decided to move to a farmhouse in Burlington, about twenty miles away, he decided to stay behind. Whitman had never been entirely comfortable at Stevens Street—he tended to get along better with Louisa than George, who never really understood the literary life. But his brother was angry at him for not coming along, and the strain in their relationship proved permanent.[122] The house Whitman bought on Mickle Street was around the corner from where he had lived for the past eleven years, and it was there he would reside until his death eight years later. Whitman was fortunate in that a widowed neighbor of his, Ann Oakes Davis, helped him out to the point of living in the house rent-free in exchange for serving as his housekeeper. Whitman also acquired a young acolyte named Horace

POETIC: A 1890 photo of Mickle Street in Camden when Whitman lived there. His house is the shorter building on the right. *Library of Congress.*

Traubel who visited him regularly, took careful notes and eventually published a multivolume biography of Whitman's final years.

Whitman continued to fret that he had not achieved success on the terms he had hoped. "I have not gain'd the acceptance of my time, but have fallen back on fond dreams of the future—anticipations," he lamented in his final years.[123] Certainly, he was not a celebrity on the scale of, say, Mark Twain. On the other hand, Whitman definitely did enjoy a higher profile than he had in his earlier—and, in truth, more artistically powerful—years of the 1850s and '60s. Though Whitman had been deemed a filthy writer during the Civil War, Democratic candidate Grover Cleveland endorsed Whitman's work during his successful campaign for president in 1884.[124] His likeness was also used by a tobacco company to sell its product. "Smoke Walt Whitman Cigars," read the text under his bearded visage. "Guaranteed Cuban Hand Made."[125]

The irony of Whitman's career is that in the last decades of the nineteenth century, he did develop a strong following, though not the kind he had most fondly imagined. As one of his best biographers, Justin Kaplan, explained, "His most fervent readers as a group were not the workingmen, artisans and farmers—the democratic leaven—whom he celebrated and addressed his poems to. They were British writers of the highest degree of cultivation." These included the brilliant Oscar Wilde (who appeared to see in Whitman a fellow queer spirit), John Burroughs, Gerard Manley Hopkins and Alfred, Lord Tennyson.[126]

A number of these people came to visit Whitman in Camden, making the city a cultural magnet for the literati. Oscar Wilde visited twice in 1882, when he was twenty-seven years old. Wilde's mother read *Leaves of Grass* to him as a child in Ireland, and he was enchanted by a figure he described "the grandest man I have ever seen. The simplest, most natural, and strongest character I have ever met in my life." (Whitman, who may have been initially skeptical, described Wilde as "a great big, splendid boy," and the two exchanged a kiss.) Wilde recorded a vivid description of Whitman in his habitat: "There was a big chair for him and a little stool for me, a pine table on which was a copy of Shakespeare, a translation of Dante, and a cruse of water. Sunlight filled the room, and over the roofs of houses opposite were the masts of ships that lay in the river. But then the poet needs no rose to blossom on his walls for him, because he carries nature always in his heart. This room contains all the simple conditions for art—sunlight, good air, pure water, a sight of ships, and the poet's works."[127]

Another British writer, Anne Gilchrist, was in a category of her own. Whitman had his share of female groupies, but none went further than Gilchrist, who declared she wanted to bear Whitman's child.[128] A widow, she relocated with her three children across the Delaware River from Camden in Philadelphia in 1876, where she remained for three years. (Ferries ran regularly between the two cities.) Whitman was initially nervous about Gilchrist and parried her advances. But he visited frequently—she kept a bedroom for him in her house—and the two remained friends after she returned in Britain until her death in 1885.

By the time he had settled in at Mickle Street, Whitman was also increasingly embraced by his famous countrymen. On May 31, 1889, a large crowd gathered at Camden's Morgan Hall (built in 1849, razed in 1955) to celebrate Whitman's seventieth birthday. Young writers like Hamlin Garland and Julian Hawthorne—son of Nathaniel and author of a series of detective novels—joined Philadelphia bankers and lawyers at the banquet. The list of people who sent in tributes included Twain, Howells and John Greenleaf Whittier, along with British luminaries such as Tennyson and Mary Smith Whitall Costelloe, who wrote, "You cannot really understand America without Walt Whitman, without *Leaves of Grass*." Whitman himself appeared in a black dinner jacket and a white shirt open at the neck, his white hair and beard forming a kind of halo.[129]

Such expressions of support were more than symbolic. As noted, publishing magnate George Childs helped Whitman buy the Mickle Street house, and industrialist Andrew Carnegie made a hefty $400 gift to Whitman.[130] Twain (who in literary terms was generally polite but kept his distance) contributed to the purchase of a fancy carriage that allowed Whitman to travel around Camden in style. Whitman also received a large donation to be used to pay for his cottage on Timber Creek, which was never constructed, though no one seemed to begrudge him over this. Even former denouncers of his work like Whittier and Thomas Wentworth Higginson, who led African American troops in the Civil War and was an early champion of Emily Dickinson, softened at the end. Higginson, who once said that Whitman's chief mistake was not in writing *Leaves of Grass* but that he did not burn it afterward, ultimately concluded that he was a genius.[131]

Inevitably, Whitman's world became smaller as he aged, and by the early 1890s, he was largely housebound. Visitors to his home found it chaotic with loose papers, though he claimed to know where everything was. He prepared a final—what came to be known as "death-bed"—edition of *Leaves of Grass* that was published shortly after he finally expired on March 26, 1892. Thousands of mourners lined the route on Haddonfield Pike as his funeral bier was taken by carriage to the elaborate tomb he had built in Harleigh Cemetery in a Camden neighborhood now known as Whitman Park. It remains a fixture of the local landscape.[132]

The Good Gray Poet took America to his heart. Now, finally, the world had taken him to heart—in Camden. "Camden was originally an accident," he noted of his decision to come there after his mother's death. "But I shall never be sorry I was left over in Camden."[133]

7

MR. EDISON GETS INDUSTRIOUS IN MENLO PARK

AN INVENTIVE ENTREPRENEUR MAKES SOUND INVESTMENTS IN LIGHT

Of the truly major events that have happened to the United States in the last 250 years, the Industrial Revolution may rank second only to the American Revolution. Literally and figuratively, New Jersey was at the center of it. The literal part is easy enough to understand. Located between the vast financial powerhouse of New York and the vast natural resource powerhouse of Pennsylvania, the Garden State was a crossroads that rapidly became an industrial state in the last third of the nineteenth century. But the figurative part is important, too. New Jersey was a hotbed of innovation, both in terms of technological development as well as economic organization, central to a gigantic transformation that would soon be shaping the nation and indeed the world.

It may be worth a little more precision in what we're talking about here. New Jersey was a principal player in the Industrial Revolution writ large, but its importance was especially apparent in what historians call the Second Industrial Revolution. The first, which began in mid-eighteenth-century England, migrated to New England at the turn of the nineteenth century, taking root in places like Pawtucket, Rhode Island, and Lawrence, Massachusetts. The First Industrial Revolution was powered by steam engines, the use of interchangeable parts in manufacturing and mass production, much of it initially done by women working in home or newly founded factories. One prominent player in this phase of the phenomenon was the Society of Useful Manufacturers (SUM), a New Jersey–sponsored private corporation founded by U.S. Treasury Secretary Alexander Hamilton. The SUM bought a parcel of land that became the city of Paterson, named after Governor William Paterson, the first planned industrial city in the nation (it became a major silk manufacturing center).

RECORD INVENTOR: Thomas Edison, with his phonograph, circa 1878. With this invention, Edison made his laboratory at Menlo Park internationally famous. *Library of Congress*.

The Second Industrial Revolution, which was kicked into high gear after the Civil War, began with the spread of railroads, large-scale steel production (for use in both transportation and building construction) and manufacturing produced by machines rather than people. Here it's important to note that it was New Jersey's *lack* of major cities relative to its immediate neighbors that was important. Dense urban areas—like Newark, the state's largest city for most of its history—could host a wide variety of industrial enterprises by virtue of the large labor force and strategic location near bodies of water, which have traditionally been key factors in the birth and growth of cities. But these very factors made the large tracts of land needed for major industrial enterprises scarce and expensive, which is why so much manufacturing in the Second Industrial Revolution was done on the urban fringe, especially since the advent of railroads gave businesses alternatives to, and even substitutions for, access to waterways (which is how cities Atlanta and Omaha could come into existence). So it was that oil refineries could spring up in Bayonne; why the Singer Manufacturing Company, famous for its sewing machines, would be based in Elizabeth; and how New Brunswick would become synonymous with rubber. To this day, New Jersey remains an intermodal transit hub with the highest rail density in the nation.[134] Its thick braids of interstate highways are more numerous than states many times its size.

But there's one more dimension to the Industrial Revolution to be considered here, and one in which New Jersey was again central: the extent to which innovation *itself* became industrialized. And at the center of *that* story is one of the most lionized, if misunderstood, figures in American history: Thomas Alva Edison. Edison is not quite rightly remembered as the inventor of a series of technologies—among them telephony (it appears Edison is the father of the word *hello*),[135] sound recording, electric lighting and motion pictures—that created modern life. To be sure, he played an important role, sometimes a decisive one, in these and other developments. But he didn't accomplish such feats single-handedly, which is very much to the point at hand. That's not simply because Edison was part of a culture of innovation that was on the way to making the United States the most powerful nation in the world. More importantly, it's because Edison refined a *methodology* of teamwork—and industrialized it—in a laboratory complex he built and supervised for a few key years in the 1870s and 1880s about thirty miles from Manhattan. It was known as Menlo Park—"the idea factory"—and he was famously known as its "Wizard." (The journalist who coined the phrase wrote a widely believed April Fool's Day spoof in which Edison's lunch was manufactured from dirt in his cellar there.) It was in Menlo Park, one might say, that modernity itself began with the work of a man who could be plausibly be said to have invented what we now call R&D: research and development.[136]

Like a lot of famous New Jerseyans surveyed in this book, Thomas Edison—known as "Al," short for his middle name of Alva—came from somewhere else. In this case, it was Ohio, by way of Canada. His great-grandfather John Edeson (as his name was spelled at the time) was a New Jersey Loyalist who fled to Nova Scotia during the American Revolution. Edison's father, Samuel, had settled in Ontario by the 1830s, where once again an Edison was on the wrong side of a revolt, this time the Mackenzie Rebellion of 1837, which led Samuel, his wife, Nancy, and their children to flee back across the border. The family settled in Milan, Ohio, a canal town about eight miles from Lake Erie, where Sam prospered as a carpenter. It was there that the couple's last and only American-born child was born in 1847.[137]

Illuminating: Exterior of the Thomas Edison Center in Edison. A much larger facility is slated for the site in the late 2020s. *Jim Cullen.*

As the baby of the family (his surviving siblings were already in their teens), young Thomas Edison was doted on by his mother, who played an important role in his education. He was considered an odd child—the word *addled* was repeatedly used to describe him—because he didn't seem to react to dramatic events like setting his father's barn on fire or the death of a childhood friend who disappeared while playing in a nearby creek.[138] It would soon become clear that Edison was a child of remarkable intelligence. But with a twist: at some unrecorded point in his youth, Edison lost most of his hearing in one ear: "I haven't heard a bird sing since I was twelve years old," he later explained, a fact that would shape his relations with other people as well as the tenor of his scientific career.[139]

A key development in the boy's life was a family relocation from Milan—the canal sustaining it was dying with the advent of railroads—to Port Huron, Michigan, when Edison was seven years old. By the time he was ten he was growing vegetables and selling them in a small grocery business, using the proceeds to give a gift to his mother ($600—a considerable sum) and to build a chemical laboratory in the basement of his house. Like a lot of children, he was enchanted by trains, a passion that was fed by the nearby Chicago, Detroit and Grand Trunk Junction Railroad, which he was allowed to ride daily for free. By the time the Civil War broke out, Edison was a newsboy hawking the *Detroit Free Press* to midwesterners eager for news—and built up a grocery business on the side. He also started his own newspaper. Edison was fantastically successful, but when a chemistry experiment he was running nearly immolated a baggage car, he was summarily ejected. It would not be the last of Edison's promising business ventures to end prematurely.[140]

But he also had more than his fair share of luck. When he saved a child by snatching him from an approaching boxcar, the boy's grateful father, a local stationmaster, offered to teach Edison to become a telegraph operator. In the context of the mid-nineteenth century, learning the language of Morse Code was akin to learning computer coding in the late twentieth: a portal of opportunity. By the time he was an adolescent, Edison was traveling the country making a decent living as a telegraph operator. He was in Cincinnati when he reported, without absorbing the actual contents of the words, that President Lincoln had been assassinated.[141]

What set Edison apart from his fraternity of telegraphers was his interest in the actual machinery of telegraphy. It's worth taking a moment to emphasize how truly miraculous a technology this was when it emerged in the 1840s: For the first time, it was possible to communicate an instant message by sending electric signals along a copper wire at a speed beyond anything a human being (even a seaborne or horse-riding one) could accomplish. This was nothing short of the conquest of time and space. But it was only possible via the acquisition of a specialized language and mastery of specialized machinery. One could summarize much of Edison's subsequent career by saying it amounted to a quest to achieve more direct transmission of sights and sounds in ways that could defy death itself.

That quest began with refinements of telegraphy, whose value—in the most fundamentally economic sense of the term—was readily apparent to insiders eager to hire him. In 1869, Edison left his job as a telegrapher with Western Union in Boston to devote himself full-time to developing new products for the marketplace. It was then that he received the first of what would become over one thousand patents. A telegraph company in New York paid him to lease a shop in nearby Newark to design and build an improved machine, and in the years that followed, Edison made a series of innovations in the business that included an ability to send messages in two different directions simultaneously (duplex telegraphy) and then four messages (quadraplex telegraphy). Edison was also groping toward later technologies that would become the dot-matrix printer and automatic messaging, which would make skilled operators like himself obsolete. At this point, interest in what Edison was doing was largely confined to businessmen who saw profit in what he could create and were eager to seed him capital for a piece of any action that would follow.[142]

Over the course of the next few years, Edison stabilized his personal and professional life. He married Newark native Mary Stilwell and had three children—in a wink toward the Morse Code, his eldest child, Marion, was nicknamed Dot; his second, Thomas Edison Jr., was dubbed Dash—and built a staff that included the durably loyal and effective Englishman Charles Batchelor. He continued to operate out of Newark, with a series of five workshops around the city, which boasted a wealth of skilled machinists, many of whom were German immigrants. But he also faced challenges. One was the city's density and pollution, which gave it one of the highest mortality rates in the nation. (His first Newark business partner died of tuberculosis, as did that partner's brother.) The Panic of 1873 was hard on Edison's businesses, forcing him to contract to the point where he had to sell his house and move into an apartment. Edison took stock of his situation. And then he made an audacious move.[143]

What the young entrepreneur really wanted was the space—both as a matter of location as well as a matter of allocated time—to devote himself wholly to the work of invention. He got the financial opportunity to pursue this dream thanks to the Gilded Age robber baron Jay Gould, who provided a large chunk of cash (Western Union provided another) as an investment in telegraphy that allowed Edison to pay off his debts, indulge his family and, most important of all, establish a large, centralized laboratory. He bought a tract of land in the modern Raritan township that had been slated for a housing development. It was on a high hill overlooking Manhattan—one could see the city's famous Trinity Church in the distance—and featured about thirty houses spread out around the town, connected by boardwalk and dirt roads. There was also nearby train service to Manhattan. The hamlet was known as Menlo Park. (Amid a wave of suburban growth, it was renamed Edison in 1954.)[144]

Edison brought his father in from Michigan to help build his complex, which included an office, a library, a long laboratory building and a brick machine shop in the rear. The Edison family occupied an impressive house on the hill, and he hired a woman named Sarah Jordan to run a boardinghouse for his unmarried employees.[145] When it opened in 1876, he had created a research campus, and over the course of the next few years it would become internationally famous.

CURRENT EVENTS: Electrician's room at Edison's Menlo Park laboratory. It was his principal base of operations from about 1876 to 1882. *Wikimedia Commons*.

It was during these years that Edison's mastery of telegraphy allowed him and his assistants to hopscotch into other technologies that would have much wider applications and gain him much wider notoriety. His interest in the transmission of coded signals led him into the transmission of the human voice, which edged him into the emerging field of telephony pioneered by the Washington, D.C.–based Scotsman Alexander Graham Bell. Telephones, in turn, led him to do pathbreaking work on the phonograph, the invention that made him a celebrity.

Here again it is worth pausing to consider just how amazing a phenomenon the transmission and recording of sound was. Just as telegraphy conquered time and space with a signal, the phonograph allowed human voices to be heard without that person being present—or even alive. For those who initially experienced it, the effect could be downright eerie. And it meant that music, which could only heretofore could be heard in live performance, could now be experienced on demand—not outdoors or in a concert hall, but in the privacy of one's own home.

And if you could do that with sound, was it possible to do it with pictures? And to actually *synchronize* them? The answer, of course, was yes—and in the years that followed, Edison would be right smack in the middle of these developments, which took decades to mature.

But before that happened, Menlo Park would be ground zero for another revolution. For thousands of years, human beings had struggled to conquer darkness. The first Promethean tool, of course, was fire, which provided light and heat to resist limitations and ravages imposed by nature. But fire was also difficult to control and dangerous, and in the millennia that followed, a series of refinements, like candles, evolved to allow human beings to live and work productively and in comfort (if you could afford it). By the middle of the nineteenth century, the nation's cities were primarily illuminated by gaslight, with lamps that were individually lit and maintained. The homes of the wealthy had them, but gaslight was expensive and generated soot that could cover furniture. The creation of a safe, reliable and inexpensive mode of lighting would have revolutionary implications for the workplace as well as the home.

There had, of course, been plenty of people working on this before Edison turned his attention to it (an interest triggered by 1878 trip out west he took with chemist Henry Draper to witness a solar eclipse in Wyoming). As early as 1808, the British scientist Humphry Davy had used a battery to show how a strong current leaping across a gap created a bright arc (known as arc lighting). An alternative approach involved heating an element to the point where it grew white hot, known as incandescent light. Arc light was the easiest to produce and distribute, which is why it was used to illuminate streets, beginning in Lyon, France, in 1855. But it was very bright and difficult to control. A key innovation by Charles Brush (like Edison, a native Ohioan) made it more practical and a fixture of American cities. But it was not something easy to distribute cheaply and easily on a mass basis.[146]

Edison zeroed in on the incandescent side of the equation. He geared Menlo Park around the quest to develop what we know as an ordinary light bulb: a glass-encased vacuum that would permit safe, steady, durable and affordable light. He came up with a prototype in 1879, but it took longer to make it workable proposition on a mass basis. The hard part was finding the right material for that heating element known as a filament: a device that could carry heat without quickly burning out. Edison's team initially focused on platinum, which was expensive and proved unreliable. After a series of forays in other directions, he finally settled on bamboo to achieve a working model for ordinary indoor lighting. In ways that may be difficult to fully appreciate, this was a truly extraordinary development that we now take for granted.

By this point, Edison was an international celebrity, and Menlo Park had become a tourist destination. As its resident Wizard, he played a key role in the making of both. Edison cultivated the press—to the point of giving stock in his enterprises to reporters, a practice that was not illegal at the time—and developed an image of himself as an amiable, if tireless, tinkerer in a seemingly magical scientific workshop. (Edison was legendary for his lack of need for sleep, typically taking naps on worktables in the middle of the night, and expected his team to be similarly nocturnal.) He offered demonstrations of his innovations at Menlo Park—the "Village of Light," as newspapers described it[147]—which drew a number of onlookers, thanks in part to its convenient location by train from Manhattan. He could sometimes get himself in trouble by making promises that proved difficult or impossible to keep to the public (and, more problematically, his investors). But Edison's confidence was generally justified. Eventually, the crush of visitors became too much, and he began to screen them more carefully. He was also able to use his hearing disability selectively in avoiding conversations in which he'd rather not engage.

By the early 1880s, Menlo Park had also become a less strategically satisfying location. The light bulb, though unquestionably important, was a peg in a much larger game board involving the creation of an electrical grid that would illuminate entire cities. Edison relocated to lower Manhattan and immersed himself in the business of selling power plants that would form the core of a network of wired electrical lighting systems. He was most interested in capturing large customers like local governments, though there was also a market for wealthy individuals like J.P. Morgan, an early adopter of cutting-edge technology. Edison made progress but also encountered limits. Some were commercial. Some were technological. And some were a matter of character.

Edison understandably considered himself a savvy businessman. Indeed, as we've seen, he showed some talent for this even as a child. Certainly, he was deeply mindful of the commercial implications of the scientific work he did, which made him a rich man. But in the world of the late nineteenth century—where, in science as in so much else, specialization was increasingly king—he was simply no match for people who were more commercially sophisticated than he was. Edison's company only really began to make money when he relinquished much of the control for running it to his wunderkind secretary, Samuel Insull, who went on to run a utilities empire before it all came crashing down in the Great Depression.

Edison had more inventive competitors than Alexander Graham Bell; those competitors proceeded down parallel tracks, some of them with less friction. In the case of lighting, he squared off against George Westinghouse, who had his own bona fides as the inventor of important railroad-brake technology and was also in the lighting business. Westinghouse—allied with Edison's former employee, Nikola Tesla, hero to the twenty-first-century entrepreneur Elon Musk—favored the transmission methodology of alternating current, in contrast to that of direct current. The so-called War of the Currents raged for a while in the late 1880s and 1890s, without a clear indication of which form was better. But AC eventually prevailed, and in the series of commercial maneuvers that followed, Edison sold his interest to create a new colossus named General Electric, founded in 1892.

Finally, there was the matter of Edison's personality: he was, at heart, a tinkerer. His inventions made him a rich man but nowhere as rich as he might have been had he been more focused on developing and sustaining his discoveries on a mass basis. This was most obvious in the case of the phonograph. Having turned the idea of reproducing sound into a reality, he showed flagging interest in turning it into a commercial enterprise, which would be achieved most decisively by the Victor Talking Machine Company using the flat discs of the German American inventor Emile Berliner rather than Edison's cylinders. (Victor was based in Camden, a burgeoning industrial city that was also the home of Walt Whitman; see chapter 6.) Edison's shop played an important role in developing motion picture technology—thanks in large part to his employee W. Laurie Dickson, a pivotal figure in film projection—but Edison, who coined the term *film*.[148] was simultaneously immersed in a series of other side projects, among them mining (he did develop a successful concrete business) and national defense (he worked with the U.S. Navy during World War I).

To some extent, Edison also showed a failure of imagination. Though unquestionably a visionary, he did not appreciate the cultural implications of his scientific work. His primary interest in the phonograph was as a dictation tool for businessmen, not as a means for recording and playing music (perhaps understandable given that he was hard of hearing). Edison was far more interested in the hardware of the nascent film industry, which he saw as an educational tool, rather than the software, or content, that would be absorbed by moviegoers. The future belonged to those, notably Jewish immigrants like the Warner brothers or Adolph Zukor—founder of a little company called Paramount—who watched people watch movies and took it from there.

For his part, Edison was always happiest when he was solving a novel technical problem. That's why, after his detour to New York for the sake of the lighting business, he crossed back across the Hudson for the second half of his life. After Edison's wife, Mary, died suddenly in 1884, he subsequently married his second wife, Mina Miller Edison, in 1886. The following year, he built a new laboratory—bigger and more modern than Menlo Park—in West Orange and bought a home for his new family, which would include three more children, in the frontier suburb of Llewellyn Park. Edison would finish his life in 1931 where he began it: on the cutting edge. In New Jersey.

TO A GREAT DEGREE, Thomas Edison was the inventor of his own myth. But it was another industrial titan who turned him into a durable national icon. Henry Ford, born in 1863, was an adolescent when Edison was doing his most pathbreaking work and became a lifelong fan, as people often are with the objects of their teenage passions. Ford would go on to become a byword for American capitalism at the turn of the twentieth century with his development of the Model T—his work, like Edison's, an elegantly simple refinement of existing technologies—growing immensely rich and influential. But Ford never lost his worshipful stance toward Edison, whose friendship he carefully cultivated in ways that ranged from extravagant gifts to investing in Edison's late-in-life schemes (like a quest to develop synthetic rubber). The two would often travel together, Edison happy for the company of someone who, unlike far too many people in his life, wasn't seeking anything from him. The two shared a hatred for Wall Street and, alas, for Jews—Edison privately and Ford all too publicly.[149] As such, they were products of their time (and ours).

Above: DRIVEN: Thomas Edison and Henry Ford, 1927. In 1929, Ford re-created
Edison's Menlo Park laboratory at his Greenfield Village historical park in Michigan.
Wikimedia Commons.

Opposite: MONUMENT TO ENLIGHTENMENT: Edison Memorial Tower, built in 1937. The town,
formerly Raritan, was renamed Edison in 1954. *Jim Cullen*.

Henry Ford had famously proclaimed that "history is more or less bunk,"
but as the automotive magnate aged, he developed a nostalgic attachment
to the past. On October 21, 1929—the fiftieth anniversary of Edison's
first demonstration of the incandescent bulb, and a week before the stock
market crash that inaugurated the Great Depression—he opened Greenfield
Village, a loving re-creation of a nineteenth-century community on the cusp
of epochal change. An important feature on the landscape of Greenfield
Village was a precise replica of the Menlo Park laboratory, featuring shelves
of chemicals, tools and other paraphernalia just as they were at that pivotal
moment. You can visit the site to this day.

At the time of his death, Thomas Edison was arguably the most famous
man in America, a figure comparable to the preeminent American inventor

of the eighteenth century: Benjamin Franklin. Franklin's achievements—he too was an innovator in his experiments with electricity, and the stove he developed (and pointedly did *not* take a patent on) remained in use for over a century—were more wide-ranging than Edison's. But Edison, who largely stayed outside the emerging culture of science research universities that took root in his lifetime, was nevertheless an important figure in the making of everyday modern life. If at times his achievements have been overstated, he was nevertheless a figure of tremendous substantive and symbolic importance—and in no sense more so than way he generated the machinery of research and development in New Jersey that made the United States a great global civilization.

8

GOVERNOR WILSON MAKES PROGRESS IN TRENTON

A PRINCETON PROFESSOR CHANGES THE STATE OF AMERICAN POLITICS

S ome states in the Union, like Ohio or New York, have produced many presidents, defined in terms of a birthplace or a location where they spent a significant amount of time in their careers. Others, like Rhode Island or Utah, haven't produced any as of this writing. New Jersey has had two residents ascend to the nation's highest office. One was Grover Cleveland (1837–1908), who was born in Caldwell and died in Princeton, where he decided to retire (Cleveland is famous as the first president to serve nonconsecutive terms—he was elected in 1884 and again in 1892). The other was Woodrow Wilson, the twenty-eighth president, who served two terms between 1913 and 1921 and remains one of the more consequential figures in American history.

Wilson is unique in at least one respect: he's the only president of the United States to have made a career in academia. (Barack Obama taught law school—like most presidents, he was an attorney—but for him university teaching was a part-time gig while he served in the Illinois legislature.) It's easy to see why professors may not be a natural fit for politics: there's a widespread notion they're likely to talk *at*, not *to*, voters, with abstract notions of life that may feel remote to those of everyday citizens. In Wilson's case, this perception seemed especially plausible because he—an expert in the new field of political science—had little experience as a candidate interacting with voters before he became president. In fact, the first and only political

DEGREES OF EXCELLENCE: Woodrow Wilson as president of Princeton University, circa 1905. He had just conferred an honorary degree on Andrew Carnegie (*right*). *Wikimedia Commons.*

job he held before becoming president was governor of New Jersey, a post he held for a mere two years before winning the presidency. Yet even before that happened, he was considered presidential timber. Clearly, Wilson was an unusual man.

He was also the product of an unusual time. Wilson's political career coincided with the cresting of the Progressive Era in American history, and he was the third president, after Republicans Theodore Roosevelt and William Howard Taft, known as a progressive. New Jersey was Wilson's laboratory (the metaphor seems apt for a movement that placed great emphasis on intellectual expertise in the form of applied theory), and his term as governor proved to be a pretty good preview of the kind of president he turned out to be—until, at least, the planet blew up into a massive world war, in which Wilson proved to be a most spectacular casualty. We live in the shadow of that tragedy.

THOMAS WOODROW WILSON SPENT more of his life in New Jersey than anywhere else: about twenty-seven of his sixty-seven years. But he always considered himself a southerner, and indeed that identity was an important part of his political perspective. Wilson, known as Tommy when a child, was born on December 28, 1856, in the Shenandoah Valley town of Staunton, Virginia, the only son and third of four children. Wilson's father, Joseph, was a Presbyterian minister, and his mother, Janet Woodrow, emigrated from England as a child. Tommy was a toddler when his father moved the family to a larger pulpit in Augusta, Georgia, in 1859, on the cusp of the Civil War. Though Ohio-born, with Unionist family, Joseph Wilson was a committed Confederate, and his son's racial attitudes were strongly shaped by his childhood experiences. The Wilsons were largely spared the ravages of the conflict, since General William Tecumseh Sherman bypassed Augusta on his famous March to the Sea. The family relocated again to Columbia, South Carolina, in 1870, where young Wilson remained for the next three years until he went to Davidson College at age sixteen. But Wilson did not remain there, returning home until he resumed his education two years later, this time at the College of New Jersey, in Princeton—a favorite destination of southerners since the time of eventual president James Madison, class of 1771. Wilson, who studied history and edited a student newspaper, graduated in 1879.

Now calling himself Woodrow, Wilson enrolled in law school at the University of Virginia. In 1882, he passed the bar exam in Georgia, where he began a practice in Atlanta. But Wilson was a restless lawyer. He was fascinated by politics, but this was a difficult field to enter without independent wealth, which he lacked. He had already shown a scholarly bent in some of his writing in college and law school, but neither did this seem to offer a clear path to making a living. By this point, Wilson had married—his wife, Ellen, a native Georgian, waited for him to graduate from law school by studying at the Arts Students League of New York—and was about to start a family. He took the lesser of the two risks in following his passions, enrolling at the newly founded graduate school at Johns Hopkins—the first research university in the nation when it was founded in 1874. Wilson spent the next two years at Hopkins, eventually earning a PhD in political science. While still working on his doctorate, he was offered a job teaching in 1885 at Bryn Mawr, a women's college outside Philadelphia. That same year, his widely hailed study, *Congressional Government*, was published. In 1888, he was offered a full professorship at Wesleyan, where he spent the next two years before attaining the prize he had sought for years: a professorship at his alma mater, now increasingly referred to as Princeton.

For the next dozen years, Wilson established himself as a popular and accomplished professor (voted the most popular faculty member at the college in a student poll six years in a row).[150] By this point, he was a nationally recognized scholar of American politics, where he argued for a stronger executive branch—though a lifelong Democrat, he found much to admire in the presidency of Republican Theodore Roosevelt—and a congressional model of government that more strongly resembled European-style parliamentary democracies.

Wilson came of age professionally and intellectually in a time of great ferment in American life, when a wide variety of people from many walks of life expressed restlessness and frustration with the excesses of a newly triumphant corporate capitalism and sought to tame its excesses. For Roosevelt, this meant the government asserting its supremacy over the private sector by growing large enough to tame corporate power. Wilson, who shared such concerns, developed a political perspective that sought to limit power by decentralizing it in both the public and private sectors. In this regard, he was the heir of Democrats like Thomas Jefferson and Andrew Jackson, even as he embraced modern methods of management and expertise to achieve such ends.

At this point, however, Wilson's ideas were largely in the realm of theory. He was nevertheless an adept practitioner of academic politics. The College of New Jersey at the turn of the twentieth century was in the middle of a major transformation. It had begun, like many of the colleges in what is now the Ivy League, as a seminary to train ministers (in this case, Presbyterians). For much of the nineteenth century, the College of New Jersey had drifted into becoming a rich boys' club. The institution's formal name change to Princeton University in 1896 signaled a movement, of which Wilson was a part, to put the school in the in the forefront of American intellectual life. His speech commemorating the university's 150th anniversary, "Princeton in the Nation's Service," laid down a marker about the role of the life of the mind, not only in education but also the nation at large. "It is plain that it is the duty of an institution of learning set in the midst of a free population and amidst signs of social change, not merely to implant a sense of duty, but to illuminate duty by every lesson that can be drawn out of the past," he said.[151] Wilson's efforts as a scholar, teacher and member of the Princeton community culminated in his elevation to the presidency of the university in 1902.

Over the course of the next decade, Wilson implemented a series of reforms in the service of an educational vision that continues to animate academe today. His page on the Princeton website is notably succinct in capturing the range and depth of his achievements:

He began by creating an administrative structure—departments of instruction with heads that reported directly to him. In place of the aimless elective system, he substituted a unified curriculum of general studies during the freshman and sophomore years, capped by concentrated study in one discipline (the academic "major") during the junior and senior years. He also added an honors program for able and ambitious students. Wilson tightened academic standards so severely that enrollment declined sharply until 1907.

Supported by the first all-out alumni fundraising campaign in Princeton's history, he doubled the faculty overnight through the appointment of almost 50 young assistant professors, called "preceptors," charged with guiding students through assigned reading and small group discussion. With a remarkable eye for quality, he assembled a youthful faculty with unusual talent and zest for teaching.

In strengthening the science program, Wilson called for basic, unfettered, "pure" research. In the field of religion, he made biblical instruction a scholarly subject. He broke the hold of conservative Presbyterians over the board of trustees, and appointed the first Jew and the first Roman Catholic to the faculty.

Not everything went Wilson's way. Indeed, he suffered a significant defeat in one of the reforms he most wanted to bring about in launching a graduate school at Princeton. Wilson firmly believed the graduate students should be integrated into the fabric of the institution, mingling with undergraduates, and sought to site the construction of graduate school buildings in the heart of campus. His friend turned rival, Dean Andrew West, sought to locate graduate students on the university's periphery. The argument grew increasingly contentious until the death of a benefactor bequeathed a large gift on West's terms (though not as large as initially believed). Wilson conceded defeat amid a growing movement to oust him from the presidency.

But these weren't the only people restless with Wilson's presidency. So was the man himself. And some very intriguing possibilities were presenting themselves at a time when New Jersey, and the nation at large, were also undergoing big changes.

ACCORDING TO ITS STATE website, New Jersey became the "Garden State" when the phrase was added to car license plates in 1954, though the term is credited to an Abraham Browning of Camden, who reputedly used it while speaking at the famed 1876 Philadelphia Centennial exhibition on New Jersey Day.[152] But in reality, New Jersey had long been the quintessential industrial state. In the last third of the nineteenth century, its population had doubled to almost two million, and it ranked third in population density, much of it concentrating in the state's cities. By 1920, six of every ten urban residents were either foreign-born or the children of immigrants, and the locus of that immigration had shifted to southern and eastern Europe. These people provided the shock troops of the state's industrial base.[153]

Big-time industry meant many things, among them big-time corruption. No state in the Union was more infested by graft than New Jersey, whose government offered financial incentives to corporations allowing them to evade antitrust regulations in the hope they would be based there (eventually, this strategy would be co-opted by neighboring Delaware, now regarded as the incorporation capital of the world). The most obvious example of this was the cockpit of the Rockefeller empire, Standard Oil of New Jersey, which would eventually be brought down by the Justice Department of Roosevelt's successor, William Howard Taft. New Jersey had a nickname of "Mother of Trusts."[154]

The linchpin between business and government were party bosses, who controlled the flow of money from one to the other, who ran for office, and who got jobs when their candidates were elected as part of what was known as the patronage system. From the mid-1890s through the first decade of the twentieth century, New Jersey was under Republican control, with the state's Democratic Party divided into factions. The key figure among them was former state senator James Smith—"Sugar Jim"—of Newark, owner of manufacturing, banking, newspaper and utility interests. Smith sensed opportunity to take back that state for the Democrats, in part because of fissures within the GOP that included so-called New Idea Republicans pushing political reform at a time when Roosevelt and Taft were tussling over control of the national party. Smith was looking for a candidate who could exploit those divisions and return the Democrats to power (and get himself elected to the U.S. Senate).[155] What he needed was a candidate he could sell—and control.

Smith's friend George Harvey, a magazine publisher who was active in state politics, had the perfect candidate in mind: Wilson. Harvey felt Wilson had a lot to offer: he was a fresh face lacking in baggage who considered himself a reformer but was associated with the more conservative wing of

SHORE SUPPORT: New Jersey Governor Wilson at Sea Girt, summer home of the state's chief executive, circa 1912—the year he was elected president. *Wikimedia Commons.*

the party. Wilson, for example, was never aligned with William Jennings Bryan, the three-time Democrat candidate for president who had long represented the face of the rurally based Populist movement that had crested in the 1890s. Smith was skeptical that Wilson, whom he dubbed "that Presbyterian priest," had the experience or political touch to be a successful candidate. But Smith's minions disagreed and convinced the boss that Wilson could function as a squeaky-clean puppet. Harvey was instructed to offer him the support of the Smith machine, which Wilson accepted as long it was understood that he would be his own man, a deal the machine accepted because its leaders didn't take him too seriously. Wilson traveled to New York's Waldorf-Astoria hotel, where he gave a speech denouncing greedy bankers. The famed plutocrat J.P. Morgan shook his hand.[156]

There were those, however, who showed some uneasiness. "Dr. Wilson, there have been political reformers who, after they have been elected to office as candidates of one party or another, have shut the doors in the face of the Organization leaders, refusing to even listen to them," noted Judge Robert Hudspeth, a member of the Democratic National Committee who was the backup choice if Wilson refused the nomination. "Is it your idea that a Governor must refuse to acknowledge his party organization?"

"Not at all," Wilson replied. "I should refuse to listen to no man, but I should be very glad to hear and duly consider the suggestions of the leader of my party." *Consider* suggestions. This was not exactly the unalloyed party spirit the leaders of the Smith machine were looking for. But they decided it was close enough.[157]

Wilson proved to be an energetic candidate who traveled the state and showed surprisingly strong political skills in connecting with ordinary voters. He delivered more than fifty speeches across New Jersey's twenty-one counties, largely extemporaneously.[158] Like Barack Obama's run for U.S. Senate from Illinois in 2004, Wilson's candidacy had a presidential buzz to it even before the governor's race was fully underway. Some of this was cynical—"WALL ST. TO PUT UP W. WILSON FOR PRESIDENT" blared a headline from the *New York Journal*, a major newspaper published by the famed William Randolph Hearst, a Democrat who disliked Wilson. But a widespread sense of excitement was palpable as he barnstormed the state to packed houses. One particularly memorable moment came late in the campaign when a New Idea Republican responded to Wilson's offer to answer any questions put to him. He asked the candidate if he believed "the boss system" existed. Wilson affirmed it did but went on to state, "If elected, I shall not, either in the matter of appointments to office or assent to legislation, or in shaping any part of the policy of my administration, submit to the dictation of any person or persons, special interest or organization." He won in a landslide and moved into the governor's office in Trenton (though he continued to live in Princeton).

The Smith machine soon realized that they had a nightmare on their hands. Wilson refused to back Smith's bid for U.S. Senate, and his lack of support not only ended Smith's bid for office but also effectively ended his political career. His son-in-law, James Nugent, took leadership to machine opposition to Wilson, while his original patron, George Harvey, withdrew his support. The smart money had made a huge miscalculation.

The new governor proceeded to team up with New Idea Republicans to propose and pass a raft of progressive reforms, among them legislation for the use of the primary system to elect candidates, regulations on public utilities, and mandating employer liability for workplace accidents. This ambitious legislative program was largely passed into law during Wilson's first full year of office in 1911.

Wilson was successful in part because he was riding a national progressive tide, one that also lifted the boats of governors like Robert La Follette of Wisconsin and Hiram Johnson of California. But part of that success was also because he had real gifts in governing that came from

GOVERNING: Portrait of Woodrow Wilson as governor in the Rotunda of the New Jersey statehouse in Trenton. *Natasha Camhi.*

many years of thinking about leadership. At the core of his practice was an emphasis on collaboration and delegation. "By meeting so often with legislators, he acted as if he were one of them," his most distinguished biographer, John Milton Cooper, has noted. "By joining his party's caucus, he became its leader." The new governor's first year in office "offered the first demonstration of how readily Woodrow Wilson could translate the study of politics into the practice of politics." In this regard, New Jersey performed considerably better than its neighbor New York, where the Tammany Hall machine continued to successfully prevent the triumph of progressive reform.[159]

In those days, a term for governorship of New Jersey was three years. After Wilson's successful first year in 1911, he was well-positioned—as his would-be puppet-masters had hoped he would be—to run for president in 1912. The increasingly bitter intra-party Republican feud between Taft and Roosevelt, who left the Republicans to found a new one known as the Progressive Party, gave the Democrats their best chance in twenty years to recapture the White House. But Wilson faced plenty of competition among the Democrats, notably Speaker of the House of Representatives Champ Clark of Missouri, as well as House majority leader Oscar Underwood of Alabama (William Jennings Bryan was still in the picture as a kingmaker if not actually a candidate). In 1912, there were a few states that did pick a candidate through the now-prevalent primary system—ironically, Wilson did not do very well in them—though most were chosen in back-room bargaining at national conventions of the kind that went back to the time of Andrew Jackson almost a century earlier. It took forty-six ballots for the delegates in Baltimore that year to finally settle on Wilson—again as fresh face with the pallor of a reformer but the temperament of a moderate. His remarkable ascent continued.

The presidential race of 1912 was among the most memorable in U.S. history. Three major candidates—the incumbent Taft, former president Roosevelt and Wilson—all considered themselves progressives, an identity that crossed party lines. A fourth, Eugene Debs, ran as a Socialist (and got almost a million votes). Most observers of the time considered the real contest as between Roosevelt, who championed what he called "The New Nationalism," and Wilson, whose campaign slogan was "The New Freedom." The difference was subtle but significant: between a Republican who sought to amass power for the forces of collective good and another who sought to distribute it more democratically common good. In the end, Wilson won. Roosevelt ran the most successful third-

POWER PORTRAIT: President-Elect Wilson with three-time Democratic candidate William Jennings Bryan in Trenton, 1913. Bryan would serve as Wilson's secretary of state. *Library of Congress.*

party race in American history and would have prevailed had his votes had been combined with those of the Republican Taft. But Wilson was also a good candidate—and a lucky one. In the space of two years, he had made the leap from the Ivory Tower of Princeton to the White House. It was, and remains, a singular achievement.

THE FIRST YEAR OF Wilson's presidency was a lot like the first year of his governorship—a run of remarkable success. In 1913, he signed the Underwood-Simmons Tariff Act, which lowered duties on foreign goods, a longtime Democratic goal and part of Wilson's platform. He also signed legislation creating the modern Federal Reserve, which continues to play a major role in regulating the U.S. economy to this day. In addition to these two pieces of landmark legislation, he pushed through the Clayton Anti-Trust Act, which strengthened government power over corporate monopoly by banning price discrimination and anti-competitive mergers, as well as declaring strikes, boycotts and labor unions legal under federal law.[160] It was also on Wilson's watch in 1913 that the Sixteenth Amendment, which created the graduated income tax, went into effect. In terms of accomplishments, his only rivals for executive vigor were Franklin Roosevelt's First Hundred Days of the New Deal in 1933 and the first year of Lyndon Johnson's Great Society 1964–65.

As his presidency wore on, however, Wilson faced increasingly difficult challenges. Some were personal: he experienced a grievous blow when his wife, Ellen, died of kidney disease in 1914. Others took the form of challenges that were beyond his control, as with the unpredictable course of the Mexican Revolution, which vexed the Wilson administration and led to unwise military interventions there (as well as the Dominican Republic and Haiti) that damaged the standing of the United States in the eyes of much of Latin America. Like a lot of presidents before and since, he found himself caught between conservatives who felt he was too active and those who felt he wasn't active enough (notably advocates for women's suffrage, which Wilson characteristically cast as a state, not federal, matter, though he himself supported giving women the vote). Wilson showed some personal as well as professional resilience, as when he entered into a successful second marriage with the widowed Edith Galt, and in prevailing in a tightly contested reelection campaign against New Yorker Charles Evans Hughes, who left a seat on the U.S. Supreme Court to run on a (now united) Republican ticket that was expected to win.

The key issue in that reelection race was one that finally consumed the Wilson presidency: the First World War. When it broke out in 1914, Wilson resolutely proclaimed American neutrality, a position widely shared by most Americans. Indeed, his reelection slogan in 1916 was "He kept us out of war." But maintaining neutrality became increasingly difficult, especially in the face of unrestricted submarine warfare by Germany that threatened maritime traffic and resulted in a series of American deaths. Shortly after his second inauguration, Wilson sought and received a declaration of war from Congress and went on to lead the nation in a conflict that would establish American global preeminence. When the war ended in 1918, Wilson went abroad—the first president to do so—to negotiate a peace treaty. He was celebrated across Europe as a conquering hero.

But the second half of Wilson's second term was a disaster. From the very beginning, he made clear that he did not want the war to be one of remorseless conquest and developed a series of proposals, famously known as the Fourteen Points, to restore global peace on a sounder basis grounded in international law. The heart of this plan was a League of Nations that would try to resolve conflicts before they started and bring unilateral aggressors to heel. One problem here is that American allies England and France wanted a far more punitive peace than Wilson had in mind. Another was that many Americans themselves were dubious about the nation getting drawn into entangling alliances that could compromise the nation's sovereign independence—an issue at the time of the nation's founding and one that has been with us ever since.

A third problem was Wilson himself. Over time, he became increasingly intransigent, a rigidity that may have had a medical basis even before he suffered a crippling stroke in late 1919. Not only did his health issues—which were kept hidden by Edith Wilson, who essentially ran the country for almost a year and a half—hobble a peace treaty the United States never signed, but they also brought some of Wilson's weaknesses to the fore. His belief in delegating authority was not always coupled by care in whom he appointed to his cabinet, with the result that his overly aggressive attorney general, A. Mitchell Palmer, promoted a so-called Red Scare in the administration's name. Wilson had a notably poor record in race relations—the federal government, which had been (and would be) an important avenue of professional advancement for African Americans, was resegregated on his watch—and Wilson was conspicuously diffident in denouncing racial violence throughout his presidency. By the time he left office in 1921, he was deeply unpopular, and the progressive movement of which he had been at the vanguard had fully run its course by the time he died, without ever fully recovering from his stroke, in 1924. The nation would remain in a conservative mood until the election of Wilson's assistant secretary of the navy, Franklin Roosevelt of New York, launched the New Deal eight years later.

The rise of Woodrow Wilson from professorship to the presidency by way of the statehouse in Trenton reads a little like a fable—a political Daniel walked into the lion's den and was not only saved by his faith but also defeated those who conspired against him. There's a lot of truth to that. But over time, his remarkable good fortune did not last, and his personal weaknesses damaged his reputation. This is tragic, not simply in terms of the sad ending to a distinguished life, but more importantly because the main things Wilson stood for—good government and international cooperation—were worthy goals that remain as relevant as ever a century later. His defeats and shortcomings are to a great degree ours.

9

"ROBESON OF RUTGERS" HITS THE GRIDIRON IN NEW BRUNSWICK

A RACIAL STRIVER MASTERS THE RULES OF THE GAME— AND PROUDLY DEFIES THEM

Over the course of the last hundred years, there have been many African American musicians who have also been important activists. Opera singer Marian Anderson (1897–1993) is one. Actor/singer Lena Horne (1917–2020) is another. So are pop stars James Brown (1944–2006) and Stevie Wonder (1950–). But Paul Robeson (1898–1976) belongs at the forefront of any such gallery. Literally and figuratively, Robeson was a towering figure, not just in the sheer range and depth of his talents but also in the depths of his commitment to fight for racial justice. He was, for those who witnessed his outsized presence, unforgettable.

Unfortunately, historical memory is a perishable commodity. The life of popular culture figures typically lasts about two generations in the best of circumstances, and Robeson's circumstances were far from ideal. He was shunned by many of his contemporaries, blacklisted by the U.S. government, and forgotten by many of his peers. Many of his greatest performances as a singer and actor were unrecorded live performances on New York and London stages, though a few have been preserved in now-classic movies such as *The Emperor Jones* (1933), *Showboat* (1936) and *Othello* (1944). Robeson's hit song "Ballad for Americans," first performed on a national radio broadcast in 1939 and made into a hit single in 1940, became a national anthem for a generation, particularly for those on the left at a time when it was more unreservedly patriotic than it tends to be now. In the 1920s, Robeson was a leading figure of the Harlem Renaissance, and in the 1930s and '40s he was a household name. He continued to be one in the 1950s—but by then he was regarded with growing hostility. Robeson remained a hero to many until his death. But to this day, his memory, such as it is, remains controversial.

That's because Robeson regarded himself as an ally of the Soviet Union at the peak of the Cold War—which is to say the peak of anticommunist fervor in the United States. Though this led to misguided support for the murderous, even genocidal, Soviet dictator Joseph Stalin, Robeson did

TOP SCORES: Paul Robeson in his football uniform, circa 1919. A star scholarship student, "Robeson of Rutgers" was also an athletic legend. *Wikimedia Commons*.

so because he, along with a great many other people around the world, regarded the USSR as a legitimate counterforce against American racism and imperialism. While many of the peers who felt the way he did nevertheless felt compelled to conform to respectable opinion as a matter of convenience, safety or the esteem of their peers, Robeson was proudly defiant—and stoically paid the price. One of the things that makes this stance notable is the degree to which Robeson had for many years exercised great discipline in presenting himself as a Black person who did not threaten white people.

This was itself a remarkable achievement, in the sense that he had not only a formidable physical presence but also an even more formidable intellectual one. In addition to singing and acting, Robeson was a scholar and Ivy League–educated lawyer. Oh—and one other thing: a football player, both collegiate and professional. His gridiron career was relatively brief. But his athletic exploits were both a reflection of his character and a synecdoche of his struggle as an African American. It's worth considering how he played the game.

Paul Robeson was the product of powerful forces in African American history. His father, William Drew Robeson, of Ibo (Nigerian) heritage, was born enslaved in North Carolina. Robeson Sr. escaped from bondage in 1860, making his way to Pennsylvania and enrolling in the Union army, heading back south twice to see his mother during the Civil War. In the years that followed, he acquired degrees in theology from the all-Black Lincoln University outside Philadelphia. While there, he met Maria Louisa Bustill, a teacher at a nearby school. Her lineage, which traced back to the Bantu people of southern Africa, was more upscale than Robeson's, including Lenape and Quaker branches and ancestors who were free Blacks and active in the abolitionist movement. Robeson and Bustill married in 1878, and the couple settled in Princeton, where Robeson became the pastor of the Witherspoon Presbyterian Church, a segregated Black satellite of the white congregation there. The Robesons had eight children, six of whom survived infancy. Paul, the youngest, was born in 1898.[161]

His early childhood was difficult. Robeson was a toddler when his father was forced from his pulpit in murky circumstances in 1901, and it took him years to find a new one. He was six years old when a coal from the family's stove set his mother's dress on fire, resulting in a fatal injury. Though his siblings continued to play a role in his life—his mother's kin much less so—Robeson was largely raised by his father, a stern but loving figure. Robeson Sr. inculcated high expectations in his son, as well as careful lessons on how to make his way in a largely white world. "Climb up if you can, but always show that you are grateful," he counseled Paul. "Above all do nothing to give them cause to fear you." According to his son, Paul Robeson Jr., the boy "learned this lesson well and added his own twist—he had an affable, smiling demeanor, combined with an irresistible empathy for his peers."[162]

Robeson spent his early childhood in a racially charged community. "Less than fifty miles from New York, and even closer to Philadelphia, Princeton was spiritually located in Dixie," he later remembered. Noting that the nearby college had long been a destination for elite white southerners since the time of James Madison, Robeson noted that in his day, "Rich Princeton was white: the Negroes were there to do the work. An aristocracy must have its retainers, and so the people of our small Negro community were, for the most part, servants." After losing his ministerial post, Robeson's father worked as a coachman, driving Princeton students around town and hauling ashes from homes. Never once, Paul noted, did William "complain of the poverty and misfortune of those years."[163] When Paul's elder brother Bill was rejected from Princeton, William appealed to university president Woodrow

Wilson, who, after stony silence, finally declared that the college did not accept Black people.[164]

Things began to improve when the Robesons relocated to Westfield, about thirty-five miles northeast of Princeton. One reason for this is that Westfield was less severely segregated, and Paul began to attend racially integrated schools. Another is that William Robeson, who found work in a grocery store—he, Paul and old brother Ben lived in the attic—managed to build a small church comprised of rural Blacks from the South (he changed his affiliation from Presbyterian to African Methodist Episcopal, or AME, which tended to have a more upwardly mobile inflection than Black Baptist churches). His flock kept him supplied with food as well as care for young Paul. And then, in 1910, the family relocated again about eighteen miles southwest to Somerville, where William secured a pulpit. It was there that Paul went to high school, again in a relatively more racially relaxed environment than Princeton, though there were only about two dozen African Americans in a student body of two hundred, and Robeson faced unremitting hostility from the school principal.[165]

It was at Somerville High School that Robeson's range of talents began to flower. In addition to being an excellent student—his hovering father made sure he mastered Latin—he emerged as a singer comfortable singing a capella and able to instinctively shift keys. (Robeson's ability to sing, and evident affection for the spirituals of his childhood, would become a prominent feature of his artistry.) It was also at Somerville High where he first performed what would become his signature role of Shakespeare's Othello, albeit in a comic version. He did so as part of a fundraiser for a school trip to Washington, D.C., which Robeson could not join because no white hotel in the nation's capital would allow a Black guest. On this and other occasions, he cheerfully complied, his disciplined good cheer reassuring his peers. As biographer Martin Duberman explained, "Paul's prudent self-possession was often mistaken for nonchalance."[166]

It was as an athlete that Robeson was literally and figuratively a big man on campus. In baseball he was a catcher; in basketball he played guard. But football was his primary sport. On offense he was an unstoppable fullback and on defense a lineman well known for his ferocity as a tackler. Indeed, state officials changed the rules of the game to allow double- and triple-teaming to blunt his impact. It didn't work. Robeson often absorbed severe punishment, notably in a 1914 game against Phillipsburg, where he scored three touchdowns and endured a broken nose and collarbone. Somerville lost 24–18 in a game considered legendary in state annals.[167]

As Robeson approached graduation, he began to consider the question of college. Despite the roadblocks, there was no question he was going—the question was where. Lincoln University, the historically Black college where his father and older brother Bill had attended, seemed like a suitable destination. But in his senior year, Robeson learned about a competitive examination open to all New Jersey high school students. The winner would receive a full scholarship to attend Rutgers College, only fifteen miles away in New Brunswick. Robeson learned of the exam late and missed a preliminary test in his junior year that would have made the senior exam less daunting. He nevertheless crammed for the test and won the competition. Though it wasn't geographically far away, Robeson was clearly going places.[168]

FIRST THERE WAS HARVARD in 1636. Then William & Mary in 1693. Third was Yale in 1701. Then Penn in 1740, Princeton in 1746, Columbia in 1754 and Brown in 1764. Coming in at number eight is the place we know as Rutgers in 1766. Today, it is the state university of New Jersey. But it has a long and complicated history.

CLASSY: Old Queens, Rutgers, completed in 1825. When Paul Robeson attended the school from 1915 to 1919, it was an elite liberal arts college. *Wikimedia Commons.*

Rutgers actually began as Queen's College, named after Charlotte Mecklenburg, wife of King George III of Britain (you know, the one the colonists rebelled against). Its charter was signed by William Franklin, son of Benjamin, who sided against his father by backing Britain in the Revolution. It took until 1771 to decide that the new institution would be located in New Brunswick, itself named in honor of the original home of King George (he got a college named after him, too, which was renamed Columbia after the Revolution). After independence, the college fell on hard times, and after a merger bid with Princeton in 1793 failed, the school closed in 1795 for a dozen years. It reopened in 1807 and suspended operations in 1816. But the college got a new lease on life—and a new name—when it was renamed for Revolutionary War veteran Henry Rutgers in 1825. For the next 120 years, it was an elite liberal arts college before a series of steps turned it into the flagship of New Jersey's state university in the mid-twentieth century.[169]

When Paul Robeson arrived at Rutgers College as a scholarship boy in the fall of 1915, the school had an enrollment of about five hundred white males. He was only the third African American student to attend (Princeton still hadn't admitted any and would not do so until World War II).[170] Shortly after his arrival, he did something no Black student ever had: successfully try out for the football team. In those early days of the sport, size was not necessarily an important qualification—Rutgers was a football powerhouse, yet five members of its 1917 squad were five feet, nine inches or shorter. At six feet, two inches and 190 pounds, Robeson was head and shoulders above the rest. This did not mean his teammates embraced him, however. In his first scrimmage, they piled on, leaving him limping off the field. Robeson was tempted to quit, but after a pep talk from his brother, he took the field again. When a player stomped on his hand, an enraged Robeson on the next play slashed into the backfield, grabbed the offending ball carrier and lifted him above his head, about to smash him to the ground. The coach intervened. But that was the last of Robeson's problems with his teammates. Indeed, in days to come they would close ranks around him.[171]

This came in handy. Besides garden-variety racist abuse, Robeson had to deal with teams such as William & Mary and Georgia Tech that simply refused to play against him. In 1916, the president of Rutgers bowed to pressure to bench Robeson in a home game against Washington and Lee (because the college was celebrating an anniversary and didn't want to endanger alumni gifts).[172]

But when Robeson did get to play—offense and defense—the results were magical. Legendary football coach Walter Camp twice named Robeson to his All-American team, describing him as a "veritable superman." One sportswriter termed him a "football genius," echoing widespread opinions that "Robeson of Rutgers" was "the best all-around player on the gridiron."

Robeson's coach, Foster Sanford, described Robeson's phenomenal toughness: "Everybody went after him, and they did it in many ways. You could gouge, you could punch, you could kick. The officials were Southern, and he took one hell of a beating, but he was never hurt. He was never out of a game for injuries. He never got thrown off the field; when somebody punched him, he didn't punch back. He was just tough. He was big. He had a massive, strong body, among other things. He felt the resentment but managed to keep it under wraps."[173]

That anger was real—and durable. Decades later, Robeson's son read a newspaper account in which he revealed he really did intend to kill that early antagonist he was ready to throw on the ground. "In a quiet, measured tone that belied the emotionally intensity behind it," Paul Robeson Jr. reported, "He said, 'It's good and healthy in today's America for what people who view me as their favorite Negro to understand I might deliberately kill a lyncher.'"[174]

For the moment, however, Robeson stayed his hand. In part, that's because he had other fish to fry. His scholarship, after all, was not athletic—it was academic. And Robeson proved to be a very good student indeed. He was elected to the college literary society and was one of four students in a class of eighty to be admitted to Phi Beta Cappa in his junior year. Robeson was also a member of the debating team who won the class oratorical prize four years in a row. His peers described him as "a gentle soul" and a man of "great gentleness"; Coach Sanford, a man not known for offering praise lightly, said Robeson "does not know the meaning of conceit" and called him "one of the most likeable fellows I have ever met."[175] Such praise is indicative of something beyond mere academic prowess. It suggests impressive social skills that are all the more notable for the challenging—at best—environment in which Robeson found himself.

And then there was music. Robeson, blessed with a warm bass-baritone voice, had enjoyed singing since he was a child, and music had long been part of his extracurricular roster before he arrived at Rutgers. Now it was becoming a bigger part of his profile. Robeson joined the college glee club, though not a traveling member when the group went on tour. He sang with a stipulation that he not attend social functions after the performances—an exclusion that had long been common and which he appeared to accept without demur. When a classmate convinced him to attend a school dance, he positioned himself on the balcony and serenaded his classmates with song to wild applause.[176] It's hard to know whether to be more appalled by the racism Robeson endured or impressed by his restraint in dealing with it.

Again, pragmatism reined. He needed money to live on while at school; one of his jobs was as a porter at Grand Central Station. But he used his glee club appearances—and his football fame as "a Rugger man"—to promote private performances. As he told a reporter a decade later, "I used to hustle around, fix up a concert, and bill myself as a star attraction." Robeson would go onstage, "sing a group of songs, orate and flourish for about 20 minutes, and then sing again." The proceeds were typically in the neighborhood of fifty dollars—no small sum. "These early ventures were practically the whole of my stage training," he later explained.[177]

The arts remained a back-channel activity, however. In his senior year, Robeson was one of four students elected to the Cap and Skull Society for those who best represented the ideals of Rutgers. He was also selected as the valedictorian of his graduating class. When another student became ill, Robeson was asked by the college president to give the commencement address. Robeson said yes but indicated he would like to address a racial theme. The president agreed.

The crowd rose in salute to Robeson as he made his way toward the podium that day. The speech he gave was closer in tone to that of Booker T. Washington than W.E.B. DuBois—a later ally—but carried with it an unmistakable challenge, calling for "an ideal government" in which "injury to the meanest citizen is an insult to the whole constitution," and where "black and white shall clasp friendly hands [remember this was a time when some considered even physical contact between the races to be unseemly] in the consciousness that we are brethren and that God is the father of us all." The crowd roared in approval.[178]

Any fair-minded observer (and maybe even some non-fair-minded observers) would agree that Paul Robeson was an impressive man who was destined for success. The question was how.

THE OBVIOUS ANSWER SEEMED to be law school. Robeson did not want to be a preacher like his father or a doctor like one of his older brothers. A law degree would secure the professional status he had been groomed for, placing him squarely in what DuBois famously called "the talented tenth" who represented the best hope for collective Black advancement. Robeson won a scholarship to New York University Law School and moved to the Brooklyn neighborhood of Bedford-Stuyvesant. But he found himself uneasy with the bohemian feel of Greenwich Village, where NYU was located.

So Robeson transferred to Columbia and relocated to Harlem—landing squarely in the middle of one of the great cultural flowerings of American history: the Harlem Renaissance. In the years that followed, Robeson would rub shoulders with some of the leading lights of African American history, among them writers James Weldon Johnson and Claude McKay (DuBois was also a member of this circle), as well as white luminaries such as Carl Van Vechten and George Gershwin.[179] Robeson also met the woman who became his wife, Eslanda, a chemist at New York–Presbyterian Hospital who later went on to become an anthropologist.

Robeson would ultimately get that law degree. He also played stints of professional football for the Akron Pros and Milwaukee Badgers. But by the mid-1920s, he was underway with what would prove to be a rapid rise as a performing artist. It began with performances at church fundraisers, fraternity and sorority affairs and events for the National Association for the Advancement of Colored People (NAACP).[180] From there it was a recital in Greenwich Village and then in London, where he began appearing on West End stages. In 1924, Robeson joined the Provincetown Players, a New York–based troupe, where he performed the plays of emerging titan Eugene O'Neill, notably *The Emperor Jones*. Robeson became world famous for his role in the 1927 Jerome Robbins and Oscar Hammerstein musical *Showboat*, particularly after starring in the 1936 movie version, and his rendition of the hit song "Ol' Man River" became a generational touchstone. Performing Shakespeare's *Othello* became a signature role; his 1943 Broadway debut in that tragedy became the longest-running show of its kind at the time.[181]

Robeson also emerged as a prominent as a political activist in these years. Increasingly vocal about the nation's racial failures, he moved further to the left in his support for the Soviet Union. This was seen as acceptable, if not exactly popular, during the dark years of the 1930s and later when the Soviet Union was an American ally in the fight against the Nazis in World War II. But with the onset of the Cold War in the late 1940s, any sympathy with the Soviets specifically, and leftism generally, were increasingly seen as suspect.

Above: DRAMATIC ACHIEVEMENT: Paul Robeson (with Uta Hagen) as Shakespeare's Othello in a Broadway production of 1943–44. He performed the role in many productions. *Wikimedia Commons*.

Opposite: JUSTICE LOBBY: Interior of the Robeson Cultural Center at the Rutgers Piscataway campus. The lobby features photographs from different phases of Robeson's career. *Jim Cullen*.

By this point, however, Robeson was no longer content to be the accommodating figure he had been for much of his youth. For this he paid a heavy price. In 1950, the U.S government withdrew his passport because he was unwilling to disclaim membership in the Communist Party. The ruling was later overturned by the Supreme Court, which found it had violated his free speech rights, in 1958. At that point, Robeson went to live abroad, including countries in the Soviet bloc, before returning the United States in 1963. His career severely curtailed, he settled back in Harlem. Robeson had a sympathetic but tetchy relationship with the civil rights movement, where his leftist commitments were problematic for those seeking mainstream acceptance. He died in 1976 still a controversial figure, but one whose outsized talents were recognized and remembered. In 1969, amid the upheavals of the civil rights movement, Rutgers established a Black House—considered the first institution of its kind on a college campus—that was renamed the Paul Robeson Cultural Center three years later. In 1992, it was moved to its current location at the university's Piscataway campus. There is also a Paul Robeson Student Center on the Rutgers Newark campus and a Paul Robeson Boulevard in New Brunswick dedicated in 2019.[182]

"I am an American," Robeson declared in his 1958 book *Here I Stand*. "Across the street [in Harlem], carefully preserved as a historic shrine, is a colonial mansion that served as a headquarters for General George Washington," he noted. "The winter of the following year found Washington and the ragged remnants of his troops encamped at Valley Forge, and among those who came to offer help in that desperate hour was my great-great-grandfather. He was born a slave in New Jersey and had managed to purchase his freedom. He became a baker and it is recorded that George Washington thanked him for supplying bread to the starving Revolutionary Army."[183]

Paul Robeson was a son of New Jersey and a great American, a greatness defined in terms of character and talent. His memory bears tending.

10

MS. STREEP LEADS CHEERS IN BERNARDSVILLE

A BABY BOOM TEEN INHABITS A ROLE—AND FINDS A VOCATION

Prodigies can come from anywhere.

Even suburbia.

(Actually, suburbia is a pretty good hatchery for prodigies.)

Meryl Streep has won countless accolades in her time—among them three Academy Awards—and often has the word *greatest* attached to her name: greatest living actor, greatest American actor, greatest actor of all time. Whether or not such terms are accurate or even useful, it does seem fruitful to apply the word *prodigy* to her. Streep wasn't a *child* prodigy like, say, Mozart; her talent didn't begin to become apparent until she went to college at Vassar and, especially, the Yale School of Drama. But it was clear early on that she was not only a person of unusual ability but also someone with a tremendous, which is to say prodigious, *range* of talent—singing, acting and an often amazing gift of mimicry. (Among her many star turns was as an aged rabbi in the 2003 HBO series *Angels in America*, in which she played four different roles.) But Streep was more than just a pretty face who became a superstar in the 1970s. She's someone who has generated a tremendous body of work spanning half a century. She's a senior-citizen prodigy who continues to astound.

How did that happen?

MERYL STREEP IS A child of suburbia.[184] Suburbia has had its thoughtful critics, but for her, it appears to have functioned the way it has been most fondly imagined: as a kid-friendly place where an intact nuclear family, relative prosperity and access to the metropolis function as a garden where success and happiness twine.

Streep's timing was also fortuitous. She arrived at the dawn of the baby boom (1946–64), that demographic bulge that followed American victory in the Second World War and the huge wave of prosperity that came in its wake. Like her peer Bruce Springsteen, born three months after Streep and forty-five miles south (see chapter 11), she grew up in an age of rising expectations in a mass media culture that fed big dreams. For them, the Garden State was a greenhouse.

Mary Louise Streep was born on June 22, 1949, in Summit, New Jersey, the eldest of three children.[185] Her ancestry is mostly German; one branch of her family line goes back to William Penn. At the insistence of her father, a marketing executive at Merck pharmaceuticals, she was named after her mother, who, after her christening (as a Presbyterian), rued the decision and started calling her Meryl. The elder Mary Streep had been a commercial artist before having children and continued to work as a freelance illustrator after they were born. Streep has referred to her mother's example frequently in her work, both in gratitude as well as a source of inspiration.

Early in Meryl's childhood, the family relocated to nearby Basking Ridge, where Streep attended Cedar Hill Elementary School and then Oak Hill (a junior high at the time). In 1963, the family moved to Bernardsville in time for her to start Bernards High School, which was within walking distance. The town, part of New Jersey's so-called Wealth Belt, is about forty-five miles west of Manhattan and retains a small-town charm redolent less of a New England village than a Main Line suburb of Philadelphia. The opening of a railroad line there in 1872 made it an early vacation destination for

Meryl Streep

STAR: Meryl Streep, high school yearbook photo, 1967. Her list of activities includes homecoming queen and the National Honor Society—but not acting. *Wikimedia Commons.*

wealthy New Yorkers, and in the century the followed, migrants from the city relocated to Bernardsville Mountain, among them Jacqueline Kennedy Onassis, who owned a ten-acre estate there. The Streeps lived in a less affluent part of town but were richer than the working-class Italians who literally lived on the other side of the tracks.[186]

Both Streep's parents were musical—dad played piano, mom was a singer—and for a while it looked like her ambitions would develop along those lines. Early in Streep's adolescence, her mother began taking her into the city, where she took singing lessons from same teacher who coached opera diva Beverly Sills. By the time she was sixteen, however, Streep had decided she was not cut out to be a vocal star.[187] She nevertheless retained a beautiful singing voice that she has deployed to good effect in a number of films, among them *Postcards from the Edge* (1990), *A Prairie Home Companion* (2006) and *Mamma Mia!* (2008).

Streep's voice lessons were part of a larger cultural education that included frequent trips to the theater, musicals in particular. Still, an early love of the performing arts was only one element in the mix of a classic postwar

DREAM HOUSE: Childhood home of Meryl Streep in Bernardstown. She had a quintessentially secure—if increasingly restless—suburban adolescence there. *Jim Cullen.*

PLAYER: Meryl Streep as a cheerleader in Bernards High School, 1966. She later described it as one of her most important roles. *Wikimedia Commons*.

childhood. Her 1967 high school yearbook portrait was accompanied by a list of activities, including being named homecoming queen as well as membership in the National Honor Society. Interestingly, acting in school musicals is not on the list, despite the fact that she appeared in enough to engender envy among her rivals (a problem that would become familiar in the years that followed).[188] An observer from the future who knew who Streep would go on to become might have been hard-pressed to see the outlines of pure genius in her teen incarnation.

But that teen incarnation was Streep's first major role. Her utter mastery of it proved to be the springboard to greatness.

MERYL STREEP'S FIRST MEMORY of acting occurred when she was six years old. She was playing the Virgin Mary in a family Christmas pageant, in which her four-year-old brother Harry played Joseph and two-year-old Dana was a barnyard animal. She remembers the intensity of her focus, which had a magnetizing effect on her siblings that yelling at them to do her will never did. It was a memorable lesson.[189]

Three years later, Streep recalled taking her mother's eyebrow pencil and etching the lines of her beloved grandmother's face on her own. She felt in her bones what it was like to feel old. "I stooped, I felt weighted down, but cheerful, you know," she remembered. She made her mother take a picture, which she has cherished ever since.[190]

It was at Bernards High, however, that an incipient sense of self-conscious craft began filtering into her consciousness. "In high school, another form of acting took hold me of me," she later remembered. "I wanted to learn how to be appealing. So I studied the character I wanted to be, that of the generally pretty high school girl." To that end, she began reading magazines and cultivating a sense of fashion (to the degree her mother allowed). "I worked harder on this characterization, really, than anyone I've done since."[191]

As all artists must, Streep considered the question of audience. She realized that for her goals to be achieved, she needed to be appealing to boys and accepted by girls—"a very tricky negotiation." She noted, "The girls didn't buy it. They didn't like me. They sniffed it out—the acting."[192]

She may have been selling herself short. Streep was by all appearances a big gal on campus—a cheerleader with a football player boyfriend (not the only one). Her yearbook described her as a "pretty blonde" and "vivacious cheerleader" with "many talents."[193]

Streep's performance of her role of the long-haired, doe-eyed cheerleader convinced the most important person of all: herself. "I reached a point in senior year when my adjustment felt like me," she explained. "I had actually convinced myself I was this person....This was real, real acting."[194]

The stage on which Streep performed was a small one. "News of the sixties seemed not to reach Bernardsville," Streep biographer Michael Schulman has noted. "The place looked like something out of *Bye, Bye Birdie*. Girls wore A-line dresses down to the knees, with Peter Pan collars cinched with a small circle pin. Boys wore khakis and Madras jackets and parted their hair." Fun was a matter of a burger at the luncheonette or a movie at the local theater. There was—and still is—a Dairy Queen off Route 202.[195]

By her own admission, Streep wasn't much of a student. Smart, certainly. And good grades—she aimed high for college. But not intellectual. When she went for an interview at Bennington, an admissions counselor asked her what books she had read over the summer. Streep remembered one about dreams by the famed Swiss psychologist Carl Jung, whose name she pronounced with a J. "Please!" the counselor replied. "Yung." Streep left the interview and found her father waiting outside. "Daddy, take me home," she said.[196]

Fortunately, there were other options for a girl looking for single-sex education, top among them the so-called Seven Sisters: Barnard, Bryn Mawr, Mount Holyoke, Smith, Radcliffe, Wellesley and—Streep's choice—Vassar, where she enrolled in the fall of 1967. "My brain woke up," she said. "I became real instead of an imaginary stuffed bunny." Exposed to a wider range of people and immersed in a series of texts—some of them dramatic—her horizons expanded rapidly. Part of this was the freedom to imagine a self outside the steady frame of a male gaze. Like many of its peers, Vassar went co-ed in the late sixties, which Streep wasn't happy about. "Everybody was a miniature Abbie Hoffman in front of a swarm of adoring girls," she grumbled. "I just thought it was bullshit."[197]

Streep, for her part, focused on developing her acting talents, which were ripening at an exponential rate. She appeared in a series of plays that ranged from Molière's 1668 comedy *The Miser* to August Strindberg's 1888 classic *Miss Julie* to Bertolt Brecht's 1943 avant-garde drama *The Good Woman of Setzuan*. Streep made her professional debut in her senior year at Vassar when she starred in an off-Broadway production of Tirso de Molina's seventeenth-century tragedy *The Playboy of Seville*. After graduation in 1971, Streep joined a summer stock company in Woodstock, Vermont. The following year, she enrolled in the Yale School of Drama.[198]

It was at Yale that Streep blossomed into a full-blown prodigy. She was part of a legendary 1975 class that included future stars Sigourney Weaver and playwrights Christopher Durang and Wendy Wasserstein in what became known as the Meryl Streep Class. It was in these years that her fellow students began to use the phrase "Streep it up," which a classmate defined as "Take the stage. Own your character. Make us look at you." This was a golden age of the method actor, personified by stars such as Robert De Niro and Dustin Hoffman. But Streep resisted the notion that her performances should be a function of personal trauma or sublimation, instead relying on imagination and close observation of those around her. This included childhood figures such as her grandmother. She defused tensions—and resentment—by poking fun at herself, as when she performed Randy Newman's classic satiric song "Lonely at the Top" for a Christmas cabaret.[199]

Shortly after graduation, Streep attracted the attention of legendary Broadway producer Joe Papp, best known for establishing the Public Theater and the Shakespeare in the Park. She appeared in a dizzying array of productions and was nominated for a Tony Award for a double-bill production of the 1945 Tennessee Williams play *27 Wagons Full of Cotton* and Arthur Miller's 1955 one-act play *A Memory of Two Mondays*. Of particular note was a 1976 production of the Bard's *Measure for Measure* in which she starred with John Cazale, a rising star who appeared in a string of five Best Picture nominees—*The Godfather* (1972), *The Godfather Part II* (1974), *The Conversation* (1974), *Dog Day Afternoon* (1975) and *The Deer Hunter* (1978)— before succumbing to cancer. Streep, who was engaged to Cazale, nursed him until he died in 1978.

Streep was not particularly interested in Hollywood. In a string of stage roles over a period of two years, she'd played a nun (something she would do again in *Doubt* in 2008), a French princess, a southern belle, a Manhattan secretary, a Civil War woman, a Russian maid and a Salvation Army activist.[200] She saw herself primarily as a character actor, and while striking in her unusual looks, Streep did not fit the mold of a classic movie star. But that was about to change. It began with a small role in the 1977 drama *Julia*, starring film giants Jane Fonda and Vanessa Redgrave. The following year, Streep appeared in the ABC four-part miniseries *Holocaust*, in which she played the Gentile wife of a Jewish artist. The series, part of the golden age of broadcast television, was seen by an estimated 120 million viewers, roughly half the U.S. population.[201] But TV in these years was not particularly prestigious, and that miniseries has not figured prominently in considerations of Streep's body of work, the way, say, the second Oscar for her searing role as a Polish émigré in *Sophie's Choice* (1982) has.

The real inflection point of Streep's career was her performance in the 1978 film *The Deer Hunter*, for which she won her first Oscar for Best Supporting Actress.[202] On the surface, the role—in a male-dominated cast that featured heavyweights such as De Niro and Christopher Walken—was not particularly attractive to Streep, who took the part to be with Cazale, struggling to work in the final months of his life. Her character, a supermarket checkout girl named Linda, provides crucial ballast in the movie. We first see her on the morning of a wedding in a gaudy pink bridesmaid's dress, making breakfast for her alcoholic father. When she brings it to him, he assaults her. But Linda is not a passive victim. When we next see her, it's at the bungalow her boyfriend Nick (Walken) shares with his buddy Michael (De Niro). She asks Nick if she can stay in their place while the two are in the army and states she wants to pay them. We don't quite know what happens—we see the action through an interior window, and Nick seems to be remonstrating at the very idea of her paying—but we get the idea that Streep's quiet, willowy persona notwithstanding, she's got a spine.

In her scenes with De Niro (the two would team up again for *Falling in Love* in 1984 and *Marvin's Room* in 1996), Streep deploys a becoming facial tactic that would become a standard part of her thespian repertoire: looking directly at her acting partner, then turning her head away, her eyes cast down, sometimes rolling her eyes as she does so in moments of levity or irony (we viewers are ever-so-briefly in on the joke). What's really quite striking about this technique is that it manages to convey shyness and assertiveness simultaneously—feminine feminism, as it were. This delicate balance goes to the heart of her performance in *The Deer Hunter*, where her character is largely at the mercy of events beyond her control but still manages to quietly express herself in ways that are both moving and life-affirming.

As Streep later explained, her performance in that role was forged in Bernardsville. "I stockpiled that character from high school, and I breathed life into her again years later as Linda in *The Deer Hunter*," she recalled in a commencement speech at Barnard College of Columbia University in 2010. And though Streep would go on to play far tougher women—including her celebrated turn as Miranda Priestly (modeled on the notorious Vogue editor Anna Wintour) in *The Devil Wears Prada* (2006) and Margaret Thatcher in *The Iron Lady* (2011), for which she won her third Oscar—Linda remains close to her heart as a refracted product of her origins: "She's still part of me, and I a part of her."[203]

SMALL-TOWN GIRL: Streep (with Robert DeNiro) in *The Deer Hunter* (1978). Streep said she drew on her Bernardstown youth for the character. *Universal Pictures.*

THE GREAT PARADOX OF actors is that by pretending to be fictive people they enliven our appreciation of real ones.[204] In her 1998 appearance on the TV program *Inside the Actor's Studio*, Streep groped her way toward expressing this idea in a way that bears quoting at some length:

> *I was thinking about applying to law school and thinking that acting is a stupid way to make a living, that it doesn't do any good in the world. But I think it does, I think it does, there's a great worth in it. And the worth is in listening to people who maybe don't even exist or who are voices in your past and through you come through the work and you give them to other people. I think that giving voice to characters who have no other voice is the great worth of what we do. So much of acting is vanity. I mean, this* [appearing on the show] *feels so great to come here and sit here and have everybody clap. But the real thing that makes me feel so good is when I know I've said something for a soul, when I've presented a soul.*[205]

The arc that runs through Streep's work is one in which the lives of women have gradually improved. They get more power over control of the terms in their lives, power that begins at home but eventually moves outside it. To a great degree, such realized dreams are a substantively American ones, grounded in aspirations that finally transcend gender. But realized dreams are also surprisingly complicated ones, with unexpected consequences, ambiguities and unfinished work. Especially for women—among them women shaped by places like the New Jersey suburbs.

As her comments also suggest, Streep's progressive feminism has a powerful moral component, a belief in a living connection across time and space that binds individuals she describes as "souls," people who are more than the sum of their bodies. Sisterhood is powerful, indeed.

11

MR. SPRINGSTEEN PLAYS ON THE JERSEY SHORE

AN AMBITIOUS HIPPIE MAKES ASBURY PARK A WORLD CAPITAL FOR ROCK-AND-ROLL

In the summer of 1969, Bruce Springsteen became a beach bum. He was not quite twenty years old, a college dropout and on his own. His parents and little sister had moved to California, his middle sister had married and settled down, and he was kicked out of the house his parents had been renting in Monmouth County. So when the owner of a local surfboard factory in Wanamassa, New Jersey, offered to let him sleep there—Springsteen was a self-styled musician and had been using it as a rehearsal space—he and the members of various bands he was in occupied cots and called it home.[206]

It was an unprepossessing life in an unprepossessing place. The main reason why Springsteen relocated to Wanamassa is that for some months he had been spending time in nearby Asbury Park, especially at a hole-in-the-wall club known at the Upstage that had opened the previous year. The Asbury Park of 1969 was a dilapidated city that was a shadow of its former self: poor, a little dangerous and seething with racial tension that would erupt into riots the following year. Asbury was a second-rate Atlantic City, itself a shadow of its glory days.

Like a lot of young musicians—like a lot of young people—Springsteen had big dreams, and it was probably for the best that he couldn't fully know how implausible they really were. Sure, he was making a name for himself on the local scene. But to the extent he was a big fish, it was in a small, muddy

GROWIN' UP: Bruce Springsteen performing "Spirit in the Night," 1973. He was living in Asbury Park at the time. *ABC-TV.*

pond. And yet there was something different about this long-haired kid who lived hand-to-mouth and often slept on the beach. For one thing, he didn't fit the class profile of many hippies, whose youthful rebellion was often backed by a layer of affluence that mitigated the risk. "I was a faux hippie (free love was all right), but the counterculture stood by definition in opposition to the conservative blue-collar experience I'd had," he explained.[207] For another, he steered clear of the drug culture that was such a big part of the scene. For a third, he was fanatically committed to his music: a Type-A personality in leather and denim. But the thing that really set Bruce Springsteen apart was the sheer force of his talent—a talent that would put Asbury Park back on the map and bring glory to a marginal state (of mind).

THE JERSEY SHORE HAS long been a repository of many dreams, whether as a matter of business, domestication or leisure. But among the most powerful—if fraught—were the hopes it might become a religious refuge, an aspiration central to the founding of Asbury Park. Located about fifty miles south of Manhattan, it was founded as an abstemious resort for Methodists in 1870, where it was hoped it could function as a site of spiritual renewal. Such plans notwithstanding, Asbury Park, which was drawn into the orbit of neighboring Long Branch, rapidly evolved into a carnival resort destination for New Yorkers and Philadelphians seeking not necessarily wholesome pleasures, explored with glee by the young Stephen Crane, who began his writing career there. One key feature of Asbury Park was its Boardwalk, which attracted fun-loving visitors from the beginning its beginnings in the 1870s.

There was also a toxic undertow that grew more pronounced with time. Plagued by racial tensions—the Ku Klux Klan was a significant presence in the 1920s and beyond—Asbury began a long, slow economic decline in the wake of the Great Depression as organized crime became a feature of its urban landscape. The tourist trade, which had started out highbrow, devolved into a day-trip destination less respectable than alternatives like Coney Island or Atlantic City (which were also suffering).[208] As a child, the Springsteen family had made visits to Asbury on holiday weekends; he described it as having "faded from its onetime Victorian splendor into a deteriorating blue-collar resort." By the time he was beginning to spend significant time there as an adolescent in 1969, it was a depressed—and depressing—city. In 1970, there was a significant race riot in which much of Asbury Park went up in flames, spawning the nickname "Dark City." He watched the conflagration by climbing a nearby water tower.[209]

Ironically, it was Asbury Park's travails that made the city an attractive destination for Springsteen. "The upside of Asbury's decline was that it had become a bit of an open city," he later explained.[210] Up until this point, he had been a suburbanite in nearby Freehold, a town on the metropolitan fringe of greater New York, but in striking distance of it. Springsteen's family had deep roots in the town, whose origins extended back to the late seventeenth century, where the place name reflected the tenor of its population. The term *freeholder* referred to a person who owned a relatively small piece of land outright for agricultural use. Such people contrasted with plantation owners who controlled vast estates, urban or rural workers who were rented space, or slaves.[211]

The name Springsteen is actually Dutch, and the WASP branch of his family was a sturdy one with deep roots in New Jersey. Census records indicated that a Joosten Springsteen settled in Monmouth County in the mid-seventeenth century and his heirs fought in the American Revolution and the Civil War, when an Alexander Springsteen joined the Union army. Another ancestor, John Fitzgibbon, decorated for his courage at the Battle of Fredericksburg in 1862, owned a house on the very street Springsteen would inhabit almost a century later. As his Fitzgibbon name suggests, the Springsteens had intermarried with the rising tides of Irish arrivals, a practice that continued into succeeding generations.[212]

Springsteen's maternal line was Italian, and it was the dominant strain in his psychic makeup. His mother, Adele, figures prominently in every major account of Springsteen's life. Adele found joy in music as well as a work ethic that provided a foundation of stability amid Douglas Springsteen's stretches of unemployment and periodic rages; Springsteen later described him as suffering from schizophrenia.[213] Douglas did support his family in his irregular way, holding a series of jobs that included stints at a nearby Ford factory, a local rug mill and taxi driver, among others. But his dark moods could lead to fits of angry behavior that would bring state troopers to the house. So when he announced that he was taking his wife and youngest child west to start over, his son was relieved, if a little apprehensive, about striking out on his own.[214]

Springsteen had known since he was in high school that he wanted to be a rock musician—seeing Elvis Presley perform on *The Ed Sullivan Show* in 1956 was an epiphany—and had actually taken some steps to achieve a marginal level of economic independence playing gigs in the years that followed his graduation from Freehold High School in 1967. He had already been spending time in Asbury Park, where cheap rents made the city and surrounding areas affordable for aspiring musicians. The city's significant African American population—about 40 percent by the seventies—gave it a critical mass of Black players, some of whom, like the emerging jazz prodigy David Sancious and saxophonist Clarence Clemons, rubbed shoulders with Springsteen at the Upstage, which attracted serious local musicians, particularly those who played at its after-hours jam sessions in the building's top floor.[215]

In the late 1960s and early 1970s, a bona fide music scene began to emerge along the Asbury Park boardwalk that came to be known the "Shore Sound."[216] It had a strong rhythm-and-blues foundation, overlaid with horns. Early practitioners included the Young Rascals, best known for their hits "Good Lovin'" (1966), "Groovin'" (1967) and "People Gotta to Be Free" (1969), as well as Looking Glass, whose hit "Brandy (You're a Fine Girl)" topped the *Billboard* pop chart in 1972. One exemplar of the Jersey Shore sound closely associated with Springsteen is Southside Johnny and the Asbury Jukes, led by Springsteen's friend and collaborator Steve van Zandt (another Italian with a Dutch name). The Asbury Park musical scene was the anvil on which Springsteen forged his style in these protean years of his career.[217]

He did so with a kaleidoscopic array of overlapping players in a series of bands with names like Steel Mill, Child, Dr. Zoom and the Sonic Boom and, more simply, the Bruce Springsteen Band. As this last moniker suggests, Springsteen's typical role was that of bandleader, which reflected his prowess as a guitarist—really the thing he was best known for in those years—as well as a songwriter. (Child passed up an opportunity to play at Woodstock Musical Festival in 1969 because the band had another gig.)[218] Springsteen was living an improvised existence, but he was also making enough money to live on and was building a significant local reputation, one that extended as far south as Richmond, Virginia, where Steel Mill played repeatedly to large crowds.

Actually, it was getting away from Asbury Park for a while that helped him figure out his place there—and where he wanted to go. In 1970, Springsteen went out to California with Steel Mill, where he visited his parents and the band played at the famous Fillmore West nightclub. But that trip, and another he took the following year, solidified his conviction that he really needed to hone his craft on his own. This was the age of the singer-songwriter—Bob Dylan was the prototype, one followed by a series of figures that included James Taylor, Jackson Browne and women like Joni Mitchell and Carole King—and this was beginning to seem like the path of least resistance in terms of breaking into the big time, even as Springsteen continued to play, and continued to be committed, to performing as part of a team.[219]

It was his friend and former manager from the surfboard factory, Tinker West, who brokered an introduction between Springsteen and the Manhattan-based producers Jim Cretecos and Mike Appel in November 1971. Springsteen played them some songs, and they liked what they heard. The sequence of events that followed are legendary among those with even a cursory knowledge of Springsteen's career: an ingenuous kid signing a contract on the hood of a car in a dark parking lot; Appel's demand that the legendary talent scout John Hammond audition Springsteen; Hammond's astonishment about what he heard; Springsteen's signing to Columbia Records by its president, Clive Davis: it was a fable in the making.[220] But the path to superstardom was anything but smooth.

In part, that's because Bruce Springsteen was a pretty stubborn fellow. One manifestation of this was his unease with Columbia's efforts to market him as a singer-songwriter in the Dylan mold, which, Dylan's undoubted folkie influence notwithstanding, conflicted with Springsteen's desire to make a rock-and-roll record (a compromise was reached for some acoustic band accompaniment for some songs).

There was another problem: the kid insisted on his New Jersey identity. He called the album *Greetings from Asbury Park, NJ*. "The main reason I put [that title on] first album was because they were pushing for this big New York thing," he told the British music magazine *Melody Maker* a few years later. "I said, 'Wait, you guys are nuts or something? I'm from Asbury Park, New Jersey. Can you dig it? NEW JERSEY.'" Springsteen also insisted on what has become the album cover's iconic image of an old-fashioned postcard illustrated with beach and boardwalk scenes inserted in the lettering. It was Columbia policy that debut albums featured the artist's photo on the cover. But Columbia art director John Berg sided with Springsteen, forever branding Springsteen's music with a strong sense of place (and leading some to believe that he was an Asbury Park, not Freehold, native). In a visual wink, his mug appears on the back cover framed as if it's a postage stamp.[221] Springsteen had branded himself.

THE IRONY OF *GREETINGS from Asbury Park, NJ* is that there's no real Asbury Park on it. Most of the actual place names on the album come from Manhattan. There's "Does This Bus Stop on 82nd St.?" for example. A reference to Bellevue Hospital in "For You." And the sages of the subway in "It's So Hard to Be a Saint in the City," a song that he used in his auditions with Mike Appel and John Hammond. The closest direct evocation of a New Jersey location on the album is "Spirit in the Night," in a fictive name for what appears to be a composite of two locations—one of which is indeed, as the song says, off Route 88 of the Garden State Parkway, and the other at the intersection of Routes 88 and Route 9 in Lakewood, New Jersey, southeast of Asbury Park. There are also those who claim Greasy Lake was actually Lake Topanemus Pond in his birthplace (now known as Freehold Pond).[222] Yet as a musical document of its time and place, *Greetings* unmistakably bears the markings of its shaggy Jersey Shore moment in the early seventies.

In the months that followed the album's release in January 1973— it stiffed—Springsteen sought to ground his music more directly in its geographic roots. Among other things, that meant recommitting to the fuller raucous Shore Sound, especially in terms of foregrounding horns. Springsteen had not given a formal name to the band he had been leading between 1972 and 1974, but it was unofficially known as the E Street Band, named after the address where keyboard player David Sancious lived with his mother just south of Asbury Park in Belmar, where the band sometimes rehearsed—and, as the increasingly important saxophonist Clarence Clemons later remembered in his colorful memoir, the band was often forced to wait outside for Sancious. "This band has spent so much fucking time on this fucking street, we should call it the E Street Band," he quoted Springsteen as saying. These verbal pieces coalesced into *The Wild, the Innocent, and the E Street Shuffle*—the "wild and innocent" referred to the name of a 1959 western Springsteen watched at the time—recorded in stints between touring from May to September and released in November 1973.[223]

This time, the local references were more prominent. "Sparks fly on E Street when the boy prophet's walking handsome and hot," Springsteen sings on the opening track, firmly establishing a sense of place. Springsteen's adoptive hometown is prominently featured in what may be the album's most famous—certainly its most beautiful—song, "Fourth of July, Asbury Park (Sandy)." While the narrator is professing his devotion to the title character, it's even more clear that what he's really in love with is the teeming life of Asbury Park and its environs—dubbed "Little Eden" in the opening line and lovingly evoked with references like the real-life Madame Marie, a fortune teller on the Boardwalk whom Springsteen made world-famous in this song. Yet the very affection with which the narrator describes such figures suggests a degree of detachment from them: he can see them so clearly, and fondly, because he has a consciousness of something else by which to measure them. This becomes clear in a remarkably evocative middle verse in which the character gets trapped on an amusement park ride when his shirt gets caught on an amusement park ride: "Didn't think I'd ever get off." His diction is telling: while words like *tilt, drag* and *caught* are rendered in a voice of wistful sheepishness, there is a strong undercurrent of entrapment in them, matched by a gathering resolution to break free. "For me this boardwalk life's through," he tells Sandy. "You oughta quit this scene, too."[224]

Indeed, "Fourth of July, Asbury Park" was something of a personal valediction for Springsteen, who described it as "a goodbye to my adopted hometown and the life I'd lived there before I recorded. 'Sandy' was a composite of some of the girls I'd known along the Shore. I used the boardwalk and the closing down of the town as a metaphor for the end of a summer romance and the changes I was experiencing in my own life."[225]

FORTUNATE: Madame Marie's, home of psychic reader Marie Castello for many decades. Springsteen immortalized the site in "Sandy (Fourth of July Asbury Park)." *Wikimedia Commons.*

But he wasn't going to get out so easy. Released in November 1973, *The Wild, the Innocent, and the E Street Shuffle* performed better than *Greetings from Asbury Park, NJ*, but it was no breakout record. Springsteen's live shows in the two years that followed deepened and widened his fan base, but his standing with Columbia records was weak, especially since the executive who signed him, Clive Davis, was no longer with the label. Columbia decided not to finance a third album until he first wrote and recorded a song that had a real shot at becoming a hit.

By this point, Springsteen was living in Long Branch, just north of Asbury Park, sweating over this composition in a way he never had. One of his early champions, journalist and critic Peter Knobler, visited him at his house there and was intrigued to see a poster for *Peter Pan* over Springsteen's bed.[226] The main female character in that story is named Wendy, and she embodies enchantment as well as disillusionment in straddling real and magical worlds. Wendy, of course, became the dramatic center of the song Springsteen wrote. It was called "Born to Run."

The song, and the album of the same name, was Springsteen's breakthrough when it was released in the summer of 1975. It was, in an important sense, a document of escape. The question is where the characters of *Born to Run* were escaping—or not escaping—*from*. In terms of actual settings of particular songs, the answer is pretty clear: a series of points between Asbury Park and Manhattan—"from the shoreline to the city," in the words of "Tenth Avenue Freezeout," a thoroughfare that intersects with E Street. While not numerous, the album does make a number of specific references to local settings, including Tenth Avenue and the Circuit, a loop of Ocean and Kingsley Avenues in Asbury Park that gets mentioned in "Night." There's also "Highway 9" in "Born to Run," a multilane thoroughfare that runs through the Monmouth County of both Freehold and Asbury Park. Springsteen's ambit continues to radiate outward to the Harlem of "Jungleland," a song whose protagonist drives over the "Jersey state line," though strictly speaking it isn't possible to plot a direct route between New York City and New Jersey unless you take a bridge or tunnel (the latter of which figures as a key plot point in "Meeting Across the River"). *Born to Run* was, in many respects, an album about leaving a time and place behind.[227]

And to a great extent, Springsteen did. Now the very personification of a rock star, he went national in a literal as well a figurative sense. In the years that followed, he roamed the country—and went abroad—in a series of

WENDY'S HOUSE: Springsteen lived in this Long Branch home when writing the songs that would comprise his 1975 album *Born to Run*. *Library of Congress*.

Rocking: The Stone Pony, which opened in 1974, home for the "Shore Sound" of Asbury Park and a regular Springsteen haunt. *Library of Congress.*

tours that would burnish his legend as his performer. By 1976, he had moved inland, renting an apartment in Holmdel.[228] In the years that followed, he occupied a series of domiciles in Greater New York. But he had left Asbury Park behind.

Springsteen's artistic vision also widened considerably. Three years after the release of *Born to Run*, Springsteen followed with *Darkness on the Edge of Town*. The album was delayed by protracted legal disputes with Mike Appel, and the mood of the album that finally emerged was darker. Its ambit was also wider. While there was a reference to Asbury Park's Kingsley Avenue in the song "Something in the Night," it largely flies under the radar (it's no boardwalk, so to speak).[229] The visual iconography of the record, as well as settings that include the Utah desert, suggest that he had outgrown his Asbury Park incubator.

The city nevertheless remained close to his heart. In 1974, toward the end of his Asbury Park days, a new club opened near its boardwalk: the Stone Pony. In the decades that followed, Springsteen would become a regular in its flourishing music scene, making many surprise appearances in any number of permutations with local figures. He would also rehearse and perform at the Asbury Park Convention Center. Dark City would also continue to figure in his art. Springsteen's 2001 song "My City of Ruins" is associated with 9/11 because he performed it in the aftermath of the attacks as part of a live telethon. But its immediate inspiration was the Asbury Park of his youth.

In the twenty-first century, Asbury Park has enjoyed a revival. Between 2000 and 2016, the percentage of homes with incomes exceeding $100,000 tripled, and the *New York Times* described it as "a seaside city reborn" in a 2019 profile. But about a third of its population still lived below the poverty line, suggesting that its recovery has been fitful.[230]

Nevertheless, its place on the imaginative map of the United States seems secure for some time to come, taking its place besides Elvis Presley's Memphis or the Beatles' Liverpool. Bruce Springsteen sculpted a life for himself at a surfboard factory on the Shore. And we're still listening to the waves.

12

WHITNEY HOUSTON GOES TO CHURCH IN NEWARK (FROM EAST ORANGE)

A DIVINELY GIFTED JERSEY GIRL EMBODIES HISTORIES OF BLACK AMERICA

T he stately brick New Hope Baptist Church sits on Sussex Avenue in Newark, just off Dr. Martin Luther King Jr. Boulevard in the city's University Heights Neighborhood (so named for its cluster of four campuses in the city: Rutgers University, the New Jersey Institute of Technology, New Jersey Medical School and Essex County College). The congregation was first organized in 1902 by two sisters who founded a Sunday school in the city, and the current structure went up eleven years later. In 1954, a new member of the church, Cissy Houston, organized a choir there. It was there, as a five-year-old, that Houston's daughter first started singing with the group, graduating to junior soloist at age eleven. Cissy Houston was a professional singer, and it was during those Sunday services that she realized her child could be one, too. So it was that one of the great musical careers of the last century was born in the chancel of a New Jersey church.[231]

By the time of her tragic death in 2012, Whitney Houston had spent a quarter of a century at the center of the nation's media culture, initially as an incandescent figure of unparalleled beauty and talent and finally as a disastrous cautionary tale of addiction. But celebrity narratives and the rapid obsolescence built into popular culture obscures the historical resonances of her remarkable life. Houston's biography sits at the intersection of a series of narratives in African American history, among them the storied traditions of the Black church, the Great Migration and the complex trajectory of upward mobility for many African Americans in the late twentieth and early twenty-first centuries. By situating her career by these coordinates, we can more fully appreciate Houston's achievements and mourn her loss. Here, truly, was a quintessential American life.

This particular story begins with Nitcholas Auther Drinkard, a third-generation farmer near the Chattahoochee River in Early County, Georgia. "Nitch," as he was known, was born in 1895, and as a young man, he raised sugarcane, peanuts, corn and sweet potatoes on his own land—until it was repossessed by county officials, an all too familiar tale in the age of the Reconstruction South. Drinkard gathered up his parents, wife and three children (there would be five more) and made his way north to Newark just after the First World War.[232]

The Drinkard family was thus at the leading edge of one of the great demographic dramas of American history. Between 1910 and 1970, six million African Americans left the region, a massive internal migration from South to North and from country to city. The Drinkards were part of the first, more rural of two waves from 1910 to 1940; another followed from 1940 to 1970.[233]

Drinkard's destination—Newark—was also paradigmatic. Between 1910 and 1930, the African American population of New Jersey grew by 132 percent, more than any other northern state, giving it the nickname "Georgia of the North." Newark was the most popular destination for the migrants, appealing for its relative lack of racism and integrated public schools (though white resistance increased as Black numbers grew).[234] Nitch Drinkard,

Thank God: New Hope Baptist Church in Newark. Gospel music was the foundation of Whitney Houston's talent. *Wikimedia Commons.*

now a factory worker whose father and grandmother had preached at his local African Method Episcopal Church in Georgia, was a pious man and a devotee of the internationally famous Fisk Gospel Singers. So he was pleased and encouraged when four of his children formed a singing group, the Drinkard Singers, to spread the gospel.[235]

Drinkard's youngest child, Emily, was born in 1933 in Newark. Like her older sister Lee, mother of the famed pop singer Dionne Warwick, Emily—whose nickname was Cissy—was a talented and ambitious member of the Drinkard Singers. But the act needed to navigate the tension between sacred and secular imperatives, toggling between performances at church sites like New Hope Baptist and making professional appearances on records and on television. In 1955, Cissy married a man named Freddie Garland, with whom she would have a son, Gary, who went on to become an NBA basketball player for the Denver Nuggets. That marriage ended in divorce; two years later, she married John Houston, a Newark politico who would go on to work as head of central planning and zoning for Mayor Kenneth Gibson, the first African American to be elected to that post in a northeastern city (1970–86). The couple had two children, Michael (born in 1961) and Whitney (born in 1963), whose nickname was "Nippy."

The Houston household was a busy one. In addition to her family and church responsibilities, Cissy had a busy recording career that included singing on records of Wilson Pickett, Elvis Presley, Paul Simon, Bette Midler, Carly Simon, Luther Vandross and many others.[236] Of particular note in this context is Aretha Franklin, whom young Whitney would refer to as "Auntie Ree," a reference to Franklin's nickname. In addition to her niece Dionne Warwick, Cissy was also the cousin of opera singer Leontyne Price on her mother's side, all of which suggests the degree to which young Whitney was marinated in an exceptionally rich musical culture and heritage. There may have been an unfortunate side to this, however: the Houston children spent a lot of time away from their parents, including with Dionne's sister Dee Dee, also a pop singer, who allegedly sexually abused Whitney and her half-brother Gary.[237]

Meanwhile, Newark lurched into crisis. By the mid-1960s, it had become a minority-majority city, with white flight and a weakening tax base eroding its economic foundations. In July 1967, Newark was rocked by multiday riots of the kind that engulfed a series of American cities in the 1960s.[238] The event shook the Houstons. "I remember lying on the floor, eating off the floor with bullets flying," Houston remembered years later.[239] At that point, the family joined the exodus out of Newark, relocating to adjacent East Orange.

At this point, Whitney Houston's life intersected with yet another historical drama: suburbanization. Though East Orange is in fact a city, it was also known for its tree-lined streets, which became a magnet for an aspirational Black middle class. The family lived in the East Orange ward of Doddstown in a house with a pool and backyard. "Everybody knew everybody in town. When you moved to East Orange from Newark, it was like *The Jeffersons*, movin' on up," noted local resident Monty Applewhite, referring to the famous sitcom of the seventies and eighties. "The Cosbys of Dodd Street" is how a family friend, "Aunt" Bae, described the Houston household in East Orange, referring to another well-known Black sitcom.[240]

Whitney Houston thus spent most of her youth in a paradigmatic New Jersey suburban childhood of swimming, trips to the local McDonalds and watching TV. Her parents enrolled her in a Catholic school, Mount Saint Dominic Academy in nearby Caldwell, from which she graduated in 1981. This frame of reference would shape her taste, and audience, for decades to come.

Nevertheless, her Black church life remained central. East Orange was only about twenty blocks from Newark, and the Houstons maintained their ties to New Hope Baptist. Music formed the core of Whitney's religious life and her secular life as well. "I grew up on the church, and gospel music has always been at the center of our lives," she later explained. "It taught me a lot about singing. It gave me emotion and spiritual things, and it helped me to know what I was singing about because in gospel music, the words mean everything." Indeed, Houston's masterful phrasing—notably her manipulation of syllables central to the gospel tradition—became the hallmark of singing style. Music critic Garrick Kennedy has described Houston's marriage of melisma and pop arrangements as "the blueprint" of her success.[241]

Her adolescence was not without challenges, however. By the late 1970s, Cissy and John's marriage was on the rocks, though they didn't divorce until the 1990s (appearing in public as if they were still together for major events in their daughter's life). John was reputedly a philanderer, and Cissy had an affair with a church minister. "Whitney was very religious, and her life was built around the church—so when this happened, her life, her universe, exploded," documentary filmmaker Kevin Macdonald told *Vanity Fair*.[242]

Her sexuality was also an issue. While working as a summer camp counselor in East Orange when she was in high school, Houston befriended Robyn Crawford, a Newark resident two years her senior. According to Crawford, the two embarked on a sexual relationship, much to the dismay and alarm of family members. Though they reportedly broke off their sexual ties in 1982, Crawford remained in Houston's life for decades, both personally and professionally, serving as her creative director for two decades.[243] In a time when same-sex relationships were often closeted, and African Americans in particular frequently expressed opposition to them, Houston was forced to hide this aspect of her identity. It would be one dimension of her life, among others, that would be regarded as problematic.

For the moment, though, Houston was on a path of vertiginous ascent. Her musical aspirations were initially eclipsed by a modeling career. In 1980, when she was sixteen, Whitney was walking on the street with Cissy on the Upper West Side in Manhattan when she was sighted by a scout for the Click Modeling agency, where she signed before moving on to Wilhelmina. Houston would appear on the pages of *Cosmopolitan*, *Young Miss* and *Glamour*, as well as several print advertisements for Revlon. Though her brother Michael reported she had been bullied as a child for her light Black skin, Whitney's pallor was a source of opportunity for her amid the complex politics of colorism.[244]

Music was nevertheless Houston's primary avocation, and having a mother in the business was undoubtedly an asset in pursuing a patient but ambitious path. The key music industry figure in Houston's professional career was record company executive Clive Davis (who also signed Bruce Springsteen; see chapter 11). Davis, who had been president of Columbia Records from 1967 to 1973, was forced out in a management shakeup and went on to found a new label, Arista, the following year. Though not a musician himself—he was trained as a lawyer—Davis had a knack for developing and sustaining careers, notably those of Dionne Warwick and Aretha Franklin, whom he signed to Arista in 1979. In 1983, Davis heard about Houston from an Artist and Repertoire (A&R) executive and went to see her perform at a Cissy Houston show, where Cissy gave Whitney the stage to perform "Home," a song from the 1974 musical *The Wiz*, as well as "The Greatest Love of All," a song Davis himself had commissioned for jazz singer/guitarist George Benson. Davis, floored by what he heard, was able to leverage his family connections with Houston and sign her to the label.[245]

Davis methodically built a scaffold for Houston's career that took almost two years. A key showcase was Houston's appearance on *The Merv Griffin Show* in 1983, where she performed "Home" to spellbinding effect.[246] The two spent a great deal of time choosing material and collaborators, including Jermaine Jackson of the Jackson 5 (a paramour at the time) and

JERSEY GIRL: Houston performs "The Star-Spangled Banner" at the 1991 Super Bowl in Tampa, Florida. *Wikimedia Commons*.

soul giant Teddy Pendergrass. Her first album, *Whitney Houston*, was released on Valentine's Day 1985. Though its momentum built slowly—it took fifty weeks to reach number one—the album went on to sell twenty-three million copies and become the most successful debut album in pop history. Over the course of the next three years, the album (and its 1987 successor, *Whitney*) also inaugurated a string of seven consecutive number one singles—"Saving All My Love for You," "How Will I Know?, "The Greatest Love of All," "I Wanna Dance with Somebody (Who Loves Me)," "Didn't We Almost Have It All," "So Emotional" and "Where Do Broken Hearts Go?"—on the *Billboard* pop chart, a record.[247] Thus by the late 1980s, Houston entered a pop stratosphere that included Michael Jackson, Madonna, Prince and Bruce Springsteen (also Jersey-born and bred forty miles south in Freehold).

Greater triumphs were to come in the new decade. In 1991, Houston was chosen to perform "The Star-Spangled Banner" at Super Bowl XXV in Tampa. The event was held during the Persian Gulf War against Iraq, giving it an extra charge. There had been memorable performances of the song before—Jimi Hendrix gave a hideously beautiful one protesting the Vietnam War at Woodstock in 1969, and Marvin Gaye gave a memorably improvisational reading of the song against a drum machine at the NBA All-Star Game in Inglewood, California, in 1983, a direct inspiration of Houston's. But she rendered what many regard as the greatest version ever performed, changing its time signature from 3/4 to 4/4 to allow her to stretch and change the pace of her vocals in a tour de force interpretation showcasing her remarkable range.[248] It generated a tremendous response, and all sales from the resulting single were donated to the American Red Cross. Houston's "Star-Spangled Banner" received a new lease on life in the aftermath of 9/11, with proceeds donated to first responders and victims' families.[249]

Houston reached the apex of her career in 1992 when she made her first foray into Hollywood, co-starring with Kevin Costner in *The Bodyguard*, a film about a pop star and the man assigned to protect her. The incidental aspect of their interracial romance was indicative of changing social attitudes, even if there were those with reservations about it then and since. But it was the soundtrack for *The Bodyguard* that made pop music history, moving thirty-four million copies and becoming the best-selling soundtrack of all time. The centerpiece of the album was its first single, a remake of Dolly Parton's 1974 country hit "I Will Always Love You," which Houston transformed into a recording for the ages (it spent fourteen weeks at number one on the *Billboard* chart). Interestingly, it was Costner who suggested the song's a capella opening, a forty-five-second stretch of pure vocalizing that demonstrated the astonishing delicacy, depth and sheer power of Houston's voice.

Yet even as her career was cresting, Houston was facing challenges that would prove personally trying. To some degree, her success exposed issues common to African Americans trying to retain their ties to Black culture while succeeding on mass terms. For some, Houston was a sellout. In 1987, a headline in *Time* magazine dubbed her "the prom queen of soul," which implicitly compared her diminutively with Aretha Franklin, widely known as the Queen of Soul. (Franklin's voice was earthier than Houston's sweeter one, though it would be hard to argue her instrument was less powerful.) At the 1988 *Soul Train* Awards in early 1989, the crowd booed when "I Wanna Dance with Somebody" was nominated for best video. The Reverend Al Sharpton, an incendiary figure in those days, dubbed her "Whitey" Houston and called for a boycott of her music.[250] One could legitimately wonder, for example, if the sometimes treacly synthesized keyboard arrangements common in 1980s, which sound dated now, really served her voice as well as they might have. But such racial essentialism was corrosive.

Houston dealt with it in a variety of ways. Some were personal, reflected in her 1992 marriage to Bobby Brown, a prominent figure in the musical subgenre of New Jack Swing, which fused rhythm and blues with the newly dominant idiom of hip-hop. (She met him at that *Soul Train* ceremony.) Their

HAVEN: Entrance to Houston's home in Mendham. A Newark native, she spent much of her life in New Jersey. *Wikimedia Commons.*

partnership would have musical consequences—notably in her hit 1990 album *I'm Your Baby Tonight*, which has a strong R&B character—as well as result in the birth of a daughter, Bobbi Kristina, born in 1993.

Houston also consistently maintained ties with the gospel tradition that had nurtured her at New Hope Baptist. The soundtrack to *The Bodyguard* includes "Jesus Loves Me," one of her favorite hymns. Her heritage is most evident in the soundtrack of her 1996 movie *The Preacher's Wife*, in which she stars in the title role alongside Courtney B. Vance and Denzel Washington. That record, the best-selling gospel album of all time,[251] includes traditional performances alongside more contemporary treatments of classics like "Somebody Bigger Than You and I," which features Brown, Faith Evans and other luminaries in a piece with a light hip-hop overlay. Gospel music would remain a pillar of her live performances.

But there was a slow deterioration in Houston's power as a singer. Some of this was self-inflicted. She became an incorrigible smoker, much to Davis's dismay.[252] More serious was a deepening drug addiction. Houston had been introduced to cocaine as early as her sixteenth birthday through her brother Michael (her half brother Gary lost his career with the Denver Nuggets for failing a drug test).[253] But the stresses of her life—aggravated by enablers in her entourage that included her own family—made her life and work sharply worse by the late 1990s. Internecine financial jockeying led her father to sue her. Her longtime companion Crawford, appalled by what she was seeing, issued an ultimatum to try to save her that resulted in her expulsion from Houston's camp in 2000.[254]

Houston's career was not one of perfect decline. She rallied in 1998 to record *My Love Is Your Love*, one of the stronger outings of her career, which spawned a series of hit singles, among them "When You Believe," a smash duet with Mariah Carey that was also part of the soundtrack for the hit animated movie *The Prince of Egypt*. But she struggled in the years that followed, dividing her time between a home in Mendham, New Jersey—an affluent community west of Newark and East Orange—as well as Alpharetta, a suburb of Atlanta. A haggard Houston shocked those who saw her rehearse for a 2001 musical tribute to Michael Jackson (the two would sometime sit silently together in hotel rooms, sharing the mutual burdens of fame).[255] She gave a painful, even alarming, interview with Diane Sawyer in 2002 in which she unconvincingly denied a drug addiction by asserting crack was too low-class a drug for her.[256] The ensuing decade was one of false starts, repackaged hits and live performances where her inability to hit the high notes, literal and figurative, of her past were all too evident. The

THEY WILL ALWAYS LOVE HER: Memorial to Houston after her death. *Library of Congress.*

broadcast of a 2005 reality show, *Being Bobby Brown*, which probably would not have run without her participation—because Houston's success eclipsed that of Brown, which was a source of tension in their marriage—showed her in a tawdry light. The shimmering ingenue of the 1980s had become a shadow of herself.

Houston made one last stand. She divorced Brown in 2007, recorded a 2009 album *I Look to You* (though the accompanying tour was widely regarded as disastrous) and acted in *Sparkle*, a 2011 remake of the 1976 film about the mother of daughters in a singing group. Things were generally looking up. By this point, her mentor Clive Davis, who had left Arista, was no longer supervising her career, though he remained in touch and was still a heavyweight whose annual pre-Grammy party was a highlight of the industry calendar. For the 2012 ceremonies, Houston booked a suite at the Beverly Hilton Hotel, and on February 9, she performed "Jesus Loves Me" with her friend Kelly Price at a local nightclub. It was her final performance. Hours before Davis's party, she was found dead in her hotel bathroom. She was forty-eight years old.[257] Even more tragically, her daughter, Bobbi, died the same way seventeen months later after spending six months in a coma.

QUEEN OF THE HIGHWAY: Whitney Houston exhibit at the travel plaza honoring off the Garden State Parkway in Union. It opened in 2023. *Jim Cullen.*

IN DEATH, WHITNEY HOUSTON came home. Her funeral was held at New Hope Baptist, attended by a stellar cast of luminaries (and a penitent Al Sharpton).[258] In East Orange, her legacy lives on the Whitney E. Houston Academy on the same Dodd Street of her childhood home, in a school named after her in 1997 that she had visited regularly and organized trips for students over many years. There is also now a travel plaza named after her on the Garden State Parkway in Union.[259]

Whitney Houston lived a life of struggle and redemption, as indeed many religious, and non-religious, people do. The formative experiences of her remarkable career unfolded in New Jersey: she was a home-grown product of the Garden State. A New Jersey that was, and remains, a synecdoche for (Black) America.

CONCLUSION

THE SANDS OF TIME

Atlantic City, December 31, 1919.[260] Revelers have gathered on the Boardwalk at Babette's, a legendary supper club, to ring in a new year, a new decade—and, with a combination of disdain and derision, the Eighteenth Amendment to the U.S. Constitution. The new law, buttressed by the recently passed Volstead Act, makes the manufacture, transportation and sale of alcohol illegal, a set of regulations collectively known as Prohibition. Earlier on New Year's Eve, there had been a mock funeral procession featuring a gigantic fake bottle of "John Barleycorn" whiskey in a coffin, led by a blackface band performing a jazz version of "Battle Hymn of the Republic." Now, at the stroke of midnight, black balloons fall and the ensemble at Babette's performs a version of "Taps" before launching into a raucous rendition of "Tiger Rag," an early jazz standard. It's far from clear what Prohibition will mean—except to a group of political and business leaders who met earlier that evening to prepare for the bonanza that will result once the only way to get a drink will be via illicit means.

Not everyone regards the arrival of Prohibition as a joke or as a financial opportunity. Three nights earlier, the Atlantic City chapter of the Women's Temperance League held a meeting in Atlantic City to herald the dawn of a new era. "Liquor, thy name's delirium," intoned the leader of the chapter in a poem she had written in honor of the occasion. Behind her a sign read, "Lips that touch liquor shall never touch mine." She then introduces a special guest: the city's treasurer, Enoch L. "Nucky" Thompson.

Thompson proceeds to relate a childhood anecdote from the infamous blizzard of 1888, when, because of his father's drunkenness, he was forced

<small>CLUBBING: Postcard for Babette's, famed Atlantic City bar favored by crime boss Nucky Johnson, fictionalized in the HBO series *Boardwalk Empire*. *Wikimedia Commons*.</small>

to forage in a railroad yard for coal to heat his family's home and killed rats for his family's dinner. "Prohibition means progress," Thompson tells the women as the moral of his story. "Never again will families be robbed of their father, held hostage by alcohol. How proud I am to live in a nation which, God willing, this year will give women the right to vote." Thompson's prayers would be answered: in 1920, women did indeed get the right to vote thanks to the Nineteenth Amendment to the Constitution. And Thompson would preside over a vast urban crime empire made possible by the Prohibition he piously affirmed at the meeting. When his driver notes that the personal anecdote he had just narrated was false, he responds, "First rule of politics, kiddo. Never let the truth get in the way of a good story."

Prohibition and Babette's were real; Atlantic City remains very much so. The rest of this scenario is fictive—a scene from the Martin Scorsese–directed pilot for *Boardwalk Empire*, which ran on HBO from 2010 to 2014. The character of Nucky Thompson is modeled on the actual Enoch Johnson, who presided less colorfully over the Boardwalk from the 1910s until he went to jail in 1941. There's no one alive today who can remember the 1920s, and much of what transpires in this show's rendition of it seems remote. If there's one thing anybody who knows anything about American history knows, it's that Prohibition was a failure—and as far as most people are concerned it was a stupid idea. Women's suffrage, by contrast, seems like common sense—stupid that it hadn't happened sooner. Less well known is that the two movements proceeded in tandem, the strong supporters of one tending to be strong supporters of the other. But inconvenient facts are soon forgotten. You don't let the truth get in the way of a good story—or, in this case, stories that seem like they should be kept separate.

This book has told good stories that really are factual (or at least written in a good faith effort to be so). Truth comes in many forms, and while poetic truth certainly has its place, there is also much to be gained—as a matter of entertainment, edification or comfort—from paying attention to the historical record. In part, that's because it can't be taken for granted: history is precious precisely because it is never complete—or, amid the literal or figurative sands of time that cover it up, permanent.

Here's one more truth: New Jersey won't be around forever. (Perhaps it's more accurate to say that the place name of New Jersey won't be around forever, though geologists would also the note that the earth's surface is also subject to change, albeit one that predates, and will likely extend beyond, that of human beings.) Like so much else, New Jersey was an accident of history. There were people living here long before the United States to which it now belongs came along, and there will be people inhabiting it until the humanity itself becomes extinct.

The lives surveyed on these pages were memorable ones. But the dramas surveyed here were in many respects common ones—of struggles of identity and achievement, of love and loss—which is finally what makes them interesting. Such dramas happen in all times and places, but both time and place give them their distinctive contours—in some important sense make them special.

The hope here is that learning about these lives will ennoble your own. And that Garden State where, in one way or another, you can feel at home.

NOTES

Prologue: Founding Fathers Share a Bed in Middlesex County

1. Much of this prologue is derived from Jim Cullen, *Best Class You Never Had* (New York: Permuted Press, 2021), 67–69. The book is a year in the life of a U.S. history class.
2. The preponderance of available evidence—gleaned from a docent at the East Jersey Olde Towne site in Piscataway, where the building has been reconstructed—appears to indicate that the Franklin and Adams stayed at the Indian Queen. One reason for thinking so is that Adams made a point of staying there, even though another inn was available, when he visited in 1800.

1. Director-General Stuyvesant Crosses the Delaware

3. Richard Veit, "Setting the Stage: Archeology and the Delaware Indians: A 12,000 Year Odyssey," in *New Jersey: A History of the Garden State* (New Brunswick: Rutgers University Press, 2018), 19.
4. Russell Shorto, *The Island at the Center of the World: The Epic Story of Dutch Manhattan and the Forgotten Colony that Shaped America* (New York: Vintage, 2005), 65.
5. Shorto, *Island at the Center of the World*, 65–66.
6. Veit, "Setting the Stage," 21–22.

7. Shorto, *Island at the Center of the World*, 88–89, 114–17; Edwin Burroughs and Mike Wallace, *Gotham: A History of New York City to 1898* (New York: Oxford University Press, 1998), 68.
8. Shorto, *Island at the Center of the World*, 165–70.
9. Harry H. Kessler and Eugene Rachlis, *Peter Stuyvesant and His New York: A Biography of a Man and a City* (New York: Random House, 1959), 153.
10. Elizabeth Covart, "New Sweden: A Brief History," Penn State University Libraries, https://libraries.psu.edu.
11. Covart, "New Sweden."
12. Shorto, *Island at the Center of the World*, 277–79.
13. Shorto, *Island at the Center of the World*, 278.
14. Kessler and Rachlis, *Peter Stuyvesant and His New York*, 167.
15. Veit, "Setting the Stage," 39.

2. Reverend Edwards Keeps the Faith at Princeton

16. George Marsden, *Jonathan Edwards: A Life* (New Haven: Yale University Press, 2003), 320–29.
17. For more on the role of the Iroquois and Comanche empires, see Pekka Hämäläinen, *Indigenous Empires: The Epic Conquest for North America* (New York: Liveright, 2023).
18. Nelson R. Burr, "New Jersey: An Anglican Adventure in Religious Freedom," *Historical Magazine of the Protestant Episcopal Church* 34, no. 1 (March 1965): 3–34.
19. See "The Spider Letter" in *A Jonathan Edwards Reader*, edited by John E. Smith, Harry S. Stout and Kenneth P. Minkema (New Haven: Yale University Press, 1995), 1–8.
20. These works are included in *A Jonathan Edwards Reader*, 89–105, 57–89.
21. Gilbert Tennent, "The Danger of An Unconverted Ministry," Ligonier, https://www.ligonier.org.
22. Marsden, *Jonathan Edwards*, 212–13.
23. Jonathan Edwards, *The Life of David Brainerd*, https://www.gutenberg.org.
24. Marsden, *Jonathan Edwards*, 293–305.
25. All these works are included in *A Jonathan Edwards Reader*.
26. Marsden, *Jonathan Edwards*, 440.
27. Quoted in Marsden, *Jonathan Edwards*, 493.
28. *A Jonathan Edwards Reader*, xxxviii.
29. Marsden, *Jonathan Edwards*, 350.

30. Joseph Yannielli, "Student Origins," Princeton & Slavery, https://slavery.princeton.edu.

3. General Washington Foils Failure in Freehold

31. See, for example, the Crossroads of the American Revolution National Heritage webpage, https://www.nps.gov, and New Jersey state "Crossroads of the Revolution" website, https://revolutionarynj.org/, September 24, 2022.

32. Maxine N. Lurie, *Taking Sides in Revolutionary New Jersey: Caught in the Crossfire* (New Brunswick: Rutgers University Press, 2022), 24–26; Revolutionary New Jersey, "New Jersey and the Revolution," https://revolutionarynj.org; George Washington's Mount Vernon, "Morristown, New Jersey," https://www.mountvernon.org; National Park Service Morristown, NJ, https://www.nps.gov/morr/index.htm, February 19, 2024.

33. Mark Edward Lender and Garry Wheeler Stone, *Fatal Sunday: George Washington, the Monmouth Campaign, and the Politics of Battle* (Norman: University of Oklahoma Press, 2017), xi.

34. David McCulloch, *John Adams* (New York: Simon & Schuster, 2002), 20.

35. Thomas Paine, "The American Crisis," December 19, 1776, https://www.gutenberg.org.

36. George Washington to Lund Washington, September 30, 1776, in *Washington: Writings* (New York: Library of America, 2001), 249; George Washington to Samuel Washington, December 18, 1776, Founders Online, https://founders.archives.gov.

37. Lurie, *Taking Sides in Revolutionary New Jersey*, 30.

38. Lurie makes this point in her preface (xiii–xiv) and surveys some recent scholarship with this emphasis (3–4).

39. Lurie, *Taking Sides in Revolutionary New Jersey*, 60–67.

40. Washington to John Hancock, December 5, 1775, in *Writings*, 256.

41. The definitive narrative of these events can be found in David Hackett Fisher, *Washington's Crossing* (New York: Oxford University Press, 2004). David McCulloch also tells this story with his usual flair in *1776* (New York: Simon & Schuster, 2005).

42. On the Continental army's reorganization and Washington's role in it, see Lender and Stone, *Fatal Sunday*, 60–75, 94–96; Ron Chernow, *Washington: A Life* (New York: Penguin, 2010), 323–36.

43. Samuel Adams and John Adams quoted in Lender and Stone, *Fatal Sunday*, 26.

44. Lender and Stone, *Fatal Sunday*, 33–41; Chernow, *Washington*, 316–20; Washington to Thomas Conway, November 5, 1777, in *Writings*, 280.

45. For a balanced yet sympathetic assessment of Lee, see Phillip Papas, *Renegade Revolutionary: The Life of General Charles Lee* (New York: New York University Press, 2014).

46. Lender and Stone, *Fatal Sunday*, 110–15.

47. For a good portrait of Clinton, who reluctantly took command from Howe, see Andrew Jackson O'Shaunessy, *The Men Who Lost America: British Leadership, the American Revolution, and the Fate of Empire* (New Haven: Yale University Press, 2013), 212–46.

48. Greene quoted in Woody Holton, *Liberty Is Sweet: The Hidden History of the American Revolution* (New York: Simon & Schuster, 2021), 355.

49. Lender and Stone, *Fatal Sunday*, 201.

50. Lender and Stone, *Fatal Sunday*, 91, 187–91.

51. Holton, *Liberty Is Sweet*, 357; Lender and Stone, *Fatal Sunday*, 289, 296.

52. Lender and Stone make this case compellingly in *Fatal Sunday*, 288–90, emphasizing that Lee understood himself to be given—and exercised—cautious discretion that the circumstances warranted. A sharply more pro-Lee account can be found in Christian McBurney, *George Washington's Nemesis: The Outrageous Treason and Unfair Court-Martial of Major Charles Lee During the Revolutionary War* (El Dorado Hills, CA: Savas Beatie, 2020).

53. Holton, *Liberty Is Sweet*, 358.

54. James Thomas Flexner, *Washington: The Indispensable Man* (Boston: Little, Brown, 1974).

55. This story is told in Henry Wiencek, *An Imperfect God: George Washington, His Slaves, and the Creation of America* (New York: Farrar, Straus & Giroux, 2003).

4. Vice President Burr Commits Murder in Weehawken

56. Nancy Isenberg, *Fallen Founder: The Life of Aaron Burr* (New York: Penguin, 2008), 11.

57. Isenberg, *Fallen Founder*, 3–5; Arnold A. Rogow, *A Fatal Friendship: Alexander Hamilton and Aaron Burr* (New York: Hill & Wang, 1999), 21.

58. John Sedgwick, *War of Two: Alexander Hamilton, Aaron Burr, and the Duel That Stunned the Nation* (New York: New American Library, 2016), 9, 21; Isenberg, *Fallen Founder*, 7. The best recent biography of Hamilton is

Ron Chernow's *Hamilton* (New York: Penguin, 2004). See chapter 1 on Hamilton's origins.

59. Isenberg, *Fallen Founder*, 9–10; Rogow, *Fatal Friendship*, 24.

60. Sedgwick, *War of Two*, 72–73; Isenberg, *Fallen Founder*, 45–53.

61. Sedgwick, *War of Two*, 48, 217–19.

62. Sedgwick, *War of Two*, 103, 111–16.

63. Chernow, *Hamilton*, 190–91.

64. Sedgwick, *War of Two*, 112, 128.

65. James Parton, *Life and Times of Aaron Burr*, vol. 1 (Boston: Houghton Mifflin, 1893), 169. Emphasis in original.

66. Chernow, *Hamilton*, 192.

67. Sedgwick, *War of Two*, 270; Chernow, *Hamilton*, 585–91.

68. Rogow, *Fatal Friendship*, 214.

69. Alexander Burr to Gouverneur Morris, December 26, 1801, in Hamilton, *Writings*, ed. by Joanne Freeman (New York: The Library of America, 2001), 972.

70. Isenberg, *Fallen Founder*, 255.

71. Sedgwick, *War of Two*, xix–xx; Rogow, *Fatal Friendship*, 231–33.

72. Chernow, *Hamilton*, 697–98.

73. Isenberg, *Fallen Founder*, 257.

74. Chernow, *Hamilton*, 692.

75. Chernow, *Hamilton*, 684.

76. Chernow, *Hamilton*, 700–701.

77. Alexander Hamilton, "Statement Regarding the Duel With Burr," circa July 10, 1804, in *Writings*; Isenberg, *Fallen Founder*, 262–63.

78. Isenberg, *Fallen Founder*, 264; Chernow, *Hamilton*, 703.

79. You can see the charges at https://founders.archives.gov; on the New York charges, see Isenberg, *Fallen Founder*, 267.

80. Graham Russell Gao Hodges, "New Jersey in the Early Republic," in *New Jersey: A History of the Garden State*, edited by Maxine N. Lurie and Richard F. Veit (New Brunswick: Rutgers University Press, 2018), 97.

81. Isenberg, *Fallen Founder*, 272–73.

5. Miss Barton Founds a School in Bordentown

82. William E. Barton, *A Quiet Will: The Life of Clara Barton* (Bellevue, WA: Big Byte Books, 2015). The book includes autobiographical chunks, some of them previously unpublished, from Clara Barton herself.

83. Laurel Thatcher Ulrich, *A Midwife's Tale: The Life of Martha Ballard Based on Her Diary, 1785–1812* (New York: Vintage, 1991).

84. Barton, *Quiet Will*, 10–11.

85. Barton, *Quiet Will*, 18; Elizabeth Brown Pryor, *Clara Barton: Professional Angel* (Philadelphia: University of Pennsylvania Press, 1987), 7–8.

86. Stephen B. Oates, *A Woman of Valor: Clara Barton and the Civil War* (New York: Free Press, 1994), 6; Pryor, *Clara Barton*, 16–17; Barton, *Quiet Will*, 22.

87. Pryor, *Clara Barton*, 22.

88. Pryor, *Clara Barton*, 23.

89. David H. Burton, *Clara Barton: In the Service of Humanity* (Westport, CT: Greenwood Press, 1995), 13.

90. *Clara Barton: The Life and Legacy of the Civil War Nurse Who Founded the American Red Cross* (Wilmington, MA: Charles River Editors, 2020), n.p.

91. Pryor, *Clara Barton*, 39–46; Burton, *Clara Barton*, 15–17.

92. Barton, *Quiet Will*, 51.

93. Barton, *Quiet Will*, 51–52.

94. Barton, *Quiet Will*, 52–53; Pryor, *Clara Barton*, 53.

95. Barton, *Quiet Will*, 53–54.

96. Pryor, *Clara Barton*, 48–51.

97. New Jersey Historic Trust, "Bordentown Historic District (Clara Barton School)," https://www.nj.gov.

98. Pryor, *Clara Barton*, 52.

99. Pryor, *Clara Barton*, 52.

100. Pryor, *Clara Barton*, 53.

101. Barton, *Quiet Will*, 72.

102. Oates, *Woman of Valor*, 11–12.

103. Barton, *Quiet Will*, 79.

104. Burton, *Clara Barton*, 21.

105. Barton, *Quiet Will*, 82–83.

106. Oates, *Woman of Valor*, 4–5.

107. Oates, *Woman of Valor*, 4–6.

108. Gina Martinez, "Top Ten Deadliest Hurricanes in U.S. History," CBS News, August 17, 2023, https://www.cbsnews.com.

109. Pryor, *Clara Barton*, x–xi.

6. Mr. Whitman Buys a Home in Camden

110. David S. Reynolds, *Walt Whitman's America: A Cultural Biography* (New York: Vintage Books, 1995), 546.

111. Justin Kaplan, *Walt Whitman: A Life* (New York: Bantam, 1982), 65–66.

112. Ralph Waldo Emerson to Walt Whitman, July 21, 1855, https://www.loc.gov.

113. Amanda Gailey, "The Publishing History of Leaves of Grass," Nineteenth Century Scholarship Online, https://nines.org/exhibits/The_Publishing_History_of_Leav.

114. Griswold's review is available at the Walt Whitman Archive site, https://whitmanarchive.org.

115. Kaplan, *Walt Whitman*, 304.

116. Kaplan, *Walt Whitman*, 345–46.

117. Reynolds, *Walt Whitman's America*, 497–98; Kaplan, *Walt Whitman*, 347.

118. Reynolds, *Walt Whitman's America*, 510.

119. Gailey, "Publishing History."

120. Kaplan, *Walt Whitman*, 23.

121. Reynolds, *Walt Whitman's America*, 524.

122. Kaplan, *Walt Whitman*, 13.

123. Kaplan, *Walt Whitman*, 22.

124. Jerome Loving, *Walt Whitman: The Song of Himself* (Berkeley: University of California Press, 1999), 429–30.

125. Reynolds, *Walt Whitman's America*, 5.

126. Kaplan, *Walt Whitman*, 22.

127. Loving, *Walt Whitman*, 410–13; Kaplan, *Walt Whitman*, 539–40; Michele Mendelssohn, "When Wilde Met Whitman," Lit Hub, July 16, 2018, https://lithub.com; Library of America Reader's Almanac, "Oscar Wilde Visits Walt Whitman in Camden, New Jersey," January 18, 2011, https://blog.loa.org.

128. Kaplan, *Walt Whitman*, 328.

129. Kaplan, *Walt Whitman*, 3–4.

130. Reynolds, *Walt Whitman's America*, 5.

131. Kaplan, *Walt Whitman*, 24–25; Scott Giantvalley, "Straight Notions of Literary Propriety: Thomas Wentworth Higginson's Gradual Unbending to Walt Whitman," *Walt Whitman Quarterly Review*, April 1987, https://oa.mg/work/10.13008/2153-3695.1149.

132. Loving, *Walt Whitman*, 480.

133. Jim Beckerman, "Walt Whitman Is Our National Poet and a Gay Icon," *Courier Post*, April 22, 2019, https://www.courierpostonline.com.

7. Mr. Edison Gets Industrious in Menlo Park

134. Paul Israel, "The Garden State Becomes and Industrial Power: New Jersey in the Late Nineteenth Century," in *New Jersey: History of the Garden State*, edited by Maxine N. Lurie and Richard F. Veit (New Brunswick: Rutgers University Press, 2018), 177–78; "How New Jersey's Logistics Power the Holiday Season," *American Journal of Transportation*, December 11, 2023, https://www.ajot.com.

135. Edmund Morris, *Edison* (New York: Random House, 2019), 544. Morris's magisterial biography is highly unusual in that it is narrated backward from death to birth.

136. Paul Israel, *Edison: A Life of Invention* (New York: Wiley, 1998), 120; Randall Stross, *The Wizard of Menlo Park: How Thomas Edison Invented the Modern World* (New York: Three Rivers Press, 2007), 54–55.

137. Thomas Edison Historical Park (National Park Service), "Samuel and Nancy Elliot Edison," https://www.nps.gov; Stross, *Wizard of Menlo Park*, 3.

138. Morris, *Edison*, 618–19.

139. Morris, *Edison*, 628–30.

140. Morris, *Edison*, 583–89.

141. Morris, *Edison*, 595–96.

142. Morris, *Edison*, 499; Stross, *Wizard of Menlo Park*, 16–19.

143. Israel, *Edison*, 175; Stross, *Wizard of Menlo Park*, 17.

144. Stross, *Wizard of Menlo Park*, 20.

145. *Thomas A. Edison's Menlo Park Laboratory, Including the Sarah Jordan Boardinghouse,* (Dearborn, MI: Henry Ford Museum and Greenfield Village, 1990), 1–4, 27. See also Israel, *Edison*, 120–23.

146. Stross, *Wizard of Menlo Park*, 76–77.

147. Morris, *Edison*, 363.

148. Morris, *Edison*, 317.

149. Stross, *Wizard of Menlo Park*, 234–37.

8. Governor Wilson Makes Progress in Trenton

150. John Milton Cooper, *Woodrow Wilson: A Biography* (New York: Vintage, 2011), 67.
151. The text of Wilson's speech can be found at Wikisource, https://en.wikisource.org.
152. Official Site of the State of New Jersey, "Nickname," https://www.nj.gov.
153. Brian Greenberg, "The Progressive Era," in *New Jersey: A History of the Garden State*, edited by Maxine N. Lurie and Richard F. Veit (New Brunswick: Rutgers University Press, 2018), 203–4.
154. A. Scott Berg, *Wilson* (New York: Putnam, 2013), 189–90.
155. Berg, *Wilson*, 190; Greenberg, "Progressive Era," 205–6.
156. Berg, *Wilson*, 181–83.
157. Berg, *Wilson*, 192.
158. Berg, *Wilson*, 199.
159. Cooper, *Woodrow Wilson*, 135–36.
160. History, Art & Archives | United States House of Representatives, "The Clayton Antitrust Act," https://history.house.gov.

9. "Robeson of Rutgers" Hits the Gridiron in New Brunswick

161. Martin Duberman, *Paul Robeson: A Biography* (New York: New Press, 1989), 3–6.
162. Paul Robeson, *The Undiscovered Paul Robeson: An Artist's Journey, 1899–1939* (New York: Wiley, 2001), 7–10. This is the first of a two-volume biography, the second of which covers the years 1939 to 1976.
163. Paul Robeson, *Here I Stand* (1958; Boston: Beacon, 1971), 10; Duberman, *Paul Robeson*, 9.
164. Robeson, *Undiscovered Paul Robeson*, 5.
165. Duberman, *Paul Robeson*, 9–10; Robeson, *Undiscovered Paul Robeson*, 13.
166. Robeson, *Undiscovered Paul Robeson*, 14; Duberman, *Paul Robeson*, 13, 25.
167. Robeson, *Undiscovered Paul Robeson*, 16.
168. Robeson, *Undiscovered Paul Robeson*, 17–18.
169. Rutgers, "Royal Governor Signs Queen's College Charter," https://timeline.rutgers.edu.
170. University Archives, "African Americans and Princeton University," https://universityarchives.princeton.edu.

171. Duberman, *Paul Robeson*, 19–20.

172. Duberman, *Paul Robeson*, 22.

173. Duberman, *Paul Robeson*, 22.

174. Robeson, *Undiscovered Paul Robeson*, 23.

175. Duberman, *Paul Robeson*, 24.

176. Duberman, *Paul Robeson*, 24.

177. Duberman, *Paul Robeson*, 24.

178. Duberman, *Paul Robeson*, 26–27.

179. Robeson, *Undiscovered Paul Robeson*, 44–45; Duberman, *Paul Robeson*, 70–73.

180. Robeson, *Undiscovered Paul Robeson*, 45.

181. Folger Shakespeare Library, "Paul Robeson as Othello," https://www.folger.edu.

182. Paul Robeson Cultural Center brochure, published by Rutgers Student Affairs; on the Newark facility, see https://studentaffairs.newark.rutgers.edu; on the naming of Paul Robeson Boulevard, see Rutgers Today, "City of New Brunswick Dedicates Paul Robeson Boulevard," https://www.rutgers.edu.

183. Robeson, *Here I Stand*, 2–3.

10. Ms. Streep Leads Cheers in Bernardsville

184. This account of Streep's origins draws on Jim Cullen, *Sensing the Past: Hollywood Stars and Historical Visions* (New York: Oxford University Press, 2013), 92–93.

185. The following biographical information comes from a variety of sources, among them Diana Maychick, *Meryl Streep: Reluctant Superstar* (New York: St. Martin's Press, 1984). I also consulted Nick Smurthwaite, *The Meryl Streep Story* (London: Columbus Books, 1984) and Iain Johnstone, *Streep: A Life in Film* (London: Psychology News Press, 2009).

186. Michael Schulman, *Her Again: Becoming Meryl Streep* (New York: Harper, 2017), 15.

187. Schulman, *Her Again*, 17–19.

188. Maychick, *Meryl Streep*, 17, 19–26.

189. Meryl Streep, commencement address at Barnard College, May 17, 2010.

190. Streep, commencement address.

191. Streep, commencement address.

192. Streep, commencement address.

193. Schulman, *Her Again*, 11–28.

194. Streep, commencement address.

195. Schulman, *Her Again*, 19–21.

196. Schulman, *Her Again*, 28–29.

197. Maychick, *Meryl Streep*, 34.

198. Schulman, *Her Again*, 51–58. For a complete record of Streep's performing record, among other information, see Simply Streep—the Meryl Streep archives: www.simplystreep.com

199. Schulman, *Her Again*, 71–79, 96.

200. Schulman, *Her Again*, 171.

201. Cullen, *Sensing the Past*, 94.

202. Much of this and the ensuing paragraph draws on Cullen, *Sensing the Past*, 97.

203. Streep, commencement address.

204. This concluding section comes from Cullen, *Sensing the Past*, 119–20.

205. See Streep's 1998 appearance on *Inside the Actor's Studio*, moderated by James Lipton (Part I).

11. Mr. Springsteen Plays on the Jersey Shore

206. Peter Ames Carlin, *Bruce* (New York: Touchstone, 2012), 54–55, 63.

207. Bruce Springsteen, *Born to Run* (New York: Simon & Schuster, 2016), 117.

208. For one recent treatment of Asbury Park's history, see Daniel Wolff, *Fourth of July, Asbury Park: A History of the Promised Land*, rev, ed. (New Brunswick: Rutgers University Press, 2022). Much of this paragraph is drawn from Jim Cullen, *Bridge & Tunnel Boys: Bruce Springsteen, Billy Joel, and the Metropolitan Sound of the American Century* (New Brunswick: Rutgers University Press, 2024), 50. Much of this chapter is adapted from material in that book, though the focus on Asbury Park is distinctive.

209. Springsteen, *Born to Run*, 105; Wolff, *Fourth of July*, 115.

210. Springsteen, *Born to Run*, 105.

211. Much of this paragraph derives from Jim Cullen, *Born in the U.S.A.: Bruce Springsteen in American Life*, 3rd ed. (New Brunswick: Rutgers University Press, 2024), 17.

212. Carlin discusses Springsteen's genealogy in *Bruce*, 1–6.

213. Barack Obama and Bruce Springsteen, *Renegades: Born in the USA* (New York: Crown, 2021), 13.

214. Cullen, *Bridge & Tunnel Boys*, 41–44.

215. The preeminent chronicler of the Asbury Park scene of Springsteen's youth is Robert Santelli. See his piece "Remembering the Upstage," in *Backstreets: Springsteen—The Man and His Music*, a collection of pieces from the fanzine edited by Charles R. Cross (New York: Harmony Books, 1989), 36–40. Santelli is also the author of the keepsake volume *Greetings from E Street: The Story of Bruce Springsteen and the E Street Band* (New York: Chronicle Books, 2006). Springsteen devotes a chapter of his memoir *Born to Run* to the Upstage; see pages 104–13

216. For an overview of the Shore Sound and its best-known local practitioners, see Santelli's "Twenty Years Burning Down the Road: The Complete History of Jersey Shore Rock 'n' Roll" in *Backstreets*, 23–33.

217. Wolff, *Fourth of July*, 114–24; Cullen, *Bridge & Tunnel Boys*, 51.

218. Carlin, *Bruce*, 61.

219. Springsteen, *Born to Run*, 138, 149.

220. Cullen, *Bridge & Tunnel Boys*, 53.

221. Dan Epstein, "Inside Bruce Springsteen's *Greetings from Asbury Park, NJ*: 10 Things You Didn't Know," *Rolling Stone*, January 5, 2018, https://www.rollingstone.com; Carlin, *Bruce*, 133; Cullen, *Bridge & Tunnel Boys*, 73.

222. Rob Kirkpatrick, *The Words and Music of Bruce Springsteen* (New York: Praeger, 2007), 17; June Skinner Sawyers, *Tougher than the Rest: 100 Best Bruce Springsteen Songs* (New York: Omnibus, 2006), 10; Cullen, *Bridge & Tunnel* Boys, 75.

223. Carlin, *Bruce*, 164; Bruce Springsteen Wiki, "E Street Band," https://brucespringsteen.fandom.com; Chris Jordan, "How the E Street Band Got Its Name," *Asbury Park Press*, February 20, 2017, https://www.app.com. Springsteen explained the origins of the band's name at a "Conversation with Bruce Springsteen" event at Monmouth University in January 2017. Clemons's recollection comes from *Big Man: Real Life and Tall Tales* (New York: Grand Central Publishing, 2009), 56; Cullen, *Bridge & Tunnel Boys*, 78.

224. Cullen, *Born in the U.S.A.*, 116.

225. Bruce Springsteen, *Songs* (1998; New York: HarperCollins, 2003), 27.

226. Louis Masur, *Runaway Dream: Born to Run and Bruce Springsteen's American Vision* (New York: Bloomsbury, 2013), 47.

227. Cullen, *Bridge & Tunnel Boys*, 100–1.

228. Carlin, *Bruce*, 229.

229. Cullen, *Bridge & Tunnel Boys*, 119.

230. Wolff, *Fourth of July*, 148–49; Julie Lasky, "Asbury Park, NJ: A Seaside City Reborn," *New York Times*, May 15, 2019, https://www.nytimes.com.

12. Whitney Houston Goes to Church in Newark (from East Orange)

231. New Hope Baptist Church, https://www.newhopenewark.org; Susan Griffith, "Whitney Houston," Blackpast, https://www.blackpast.org.

232. Gerrick Kennedy, *Didn't We Almost Have It All: In Defense of Whitney Houston* (New York: Abrams Press, 2022), 51–52; Geni, "Nicholas Auther Drinkard," https://www.geni.com.

233. U.S. Census Bureau, "The Great Migration," https://www.census.gov.

234. PBS Learning Media, "The Great Migration: New Jersey Then and Now—Social Effects of the Great Migration" (video), https://ny.pbslearningmedia.org/.

235. Kennedy, *Didn't We Almost Have It All*, 52–53; Craig Harris, "Drinkard Singers Biography," Allmusic, https://www.allmusic.com.

236. Mark Bego, *Whitney Houston* (London: Plexus, 2012), 25.

237. Gary Garland makes this accusation in the notably well-made and reported documentary *Whitney*, directed by Kevin Macdonald (Miramax, 2018). For further reporting on this, see "*Whitney* Doc Alleges Singer Was Sexually Abused by Cousin Dee Dee Warwick," *Essence*, updated October 24, 2020, https://www.essence.com. Dee Dee Warwick died in 2008 before such allegations were made.

238. For one scholarly account of this event, see Kevin Mumford, *Newark: A History of Race, Rights, and Riots in America* (New York: New York University Press, 2007). For an evocative oral history of the riots on their fiftieth anniversary, see Rick Rojas and Khorri Atkinson, "Five Days That Shaped, and Haunted Newark," *New York Times*, July 11, 2017, https://www.nytimes.com.

239. Houston quoted in *Whitney* documentary.

240. John Leland, "In East Orange, Before Whitney Houston Was a Star," *New York Times*, February 16, 2012; *Whitney* documentary.

241. Kennedy, *Didn't We Almost Have It All*, 18.

242. Julie Miller, "Whitney Houston's Dark Family Secret Uncovered in New Documentary," *Vanity Fair*, May 16, 2018, www.vanityfair.com.

243. Robyn Crawford, *A Song for You: My Life with Whitney Houston* (New York: Dutton, 2019). Michael Houston is among those raising concerns about his sister's relationship with Crawford in *Whitney*.

244. Bego, *Whitney Houston*, 39–40; Michael Houston says his sister was "picked on" for her skin color in *Whitney*.

245. Clive Davis with Anthony DeCurtis, *The Soundtrack of My Life* (New York: Simon & Schuster, 2013), 308–9. Davis devotes an entire heartfelt

chapter to his professional relationship with Houston, undoubtedly the most important client in his musical career.

246. You can see her performance, and how Davis/Griffith framed it, in *Whitney*.

247. Davis and DeCurtis, *Soundtrack of My Life*, 311–18.

248. Houston's musical director Rickey Minor offers a compelling explanation of how the song was reconceptualized and performed in *Whitney*.

249. Davis and DeCurtis, *Soundtrack of My Life*, 322.

250. Richard Corliss, "The Prom Queen of Soul," *Time*, July 13, 1987, https://content.time.com/. Corliss's analysis captures the state of play in the late eighties: "To her admirers, Houston's success represents an overdue vindication of that neglected American institution, the black middle class. Here is a morality play with a happy ending: two strong, affectionate parents nurturing their talented daughter toward the show-biz dream of fame without pain. To scoffers in the rock critical Establishment, though, the 5-ft. 8-in., 115-lb. beauty is a black Barbie doll. To them, Whitney's voice, so willing to roam through the breadth of pop music, shows no emotional depth; they find the selection of her songs bland and timid." For footage of the 1988 Soul Train Awards, see https://www.youtube.com/watch?v=eHtJu19qPhg. There's footage of Sharpton in *Whitney*.

251. Davis and DeCurtis, *Soundtrack of My Life*, 328.

252. This is something Davis discusses throughout the latter stretch of his chapter on Houston; see, for example, page 338.

253. The two men describe their own addictions and their role in their sister's in *Whitney*.

254. These matters are discussed in *Whitney*.

255. *Whitney*.

256. The interview is available on You Tube, https://www.youtube.com/watch?v=vWzElaK1uqc.

257. Bego, *Whitney Houston*, 7–8; Kennedy, *Didn't We Almost Have It All*, 259–67; Davis and DeCurtis, *Soundtrack of My Life*, 339–41.

258. Steve Rose, "Not Black Enough: The Identity Crisis that Haunted Whitney Houston," *The Guardian*, July 7, 2018, www.theguardian.com; Randy Cordova, "In Revealing Documentary *Whitney*, a Superstar's Life Unravels," *Arizona Republic*, July 5, 2018, https://www.azcentral.com.

259. Eugene Paik, "Students at East Orange School Named for Whitney Houston Mourn Her Death," *Newark Star-Ledger*, February 13, 2012, https://www.nj.com.

Conclusion: The Sands of Time

260. The following four paragraphs are adapted from Jim Cullen, *From Memory to History: Television Versions of the Twentieth Century* (New Brunswick: Rutgers University Press, 2021), 1–2.

ABOUT THE AUTHOR

PERCOLATING: Starbucks coffee shop in Dobbs Ferry, New York, where this book (among others) was written.

Jim Cullen was born in Queens, New York, the son of a New York City firefighter and a homemaker. He attended Tufts University and holds a PhD in American Studies from Brown University. Jim taught at Harvard, Brown and Sarah Lawrence College before settling down for nineteenth years at the Ethical Culture Fieldston School in New York, where he served as chair of the History Department and as a member of the Board of Trustees. Since 2020, he has been a member of the faculty at the recently founded Greenwich Country Day high school in Connecticut.

Jim is the author of over twenty books, including *The American Dream: A Short History of an Idea that Shaped a Nation* (2003), *Bridge & Tunnel Boys: Bruce Springsteen, Billy Joel, and the Metropolitan Sound of the American Century* (2023) and *Born in the U.S.A.: Bruce Springsteen in American Life* (3rd edition, 2024). His work has appeared in the *Washington Post*, *Time*, *Rolling Stone*, *Newsday*, (New York) *Daily News*, CNN.com, *Forbes*, the *American Historical Review*, the *Journal of American History* and other publications. Jim lives with his wife, Sarah Lawrence College historian Lyde Cullen Sizer, in Hastings-on-Hudson, New York, right across the Hudson from the New Jersey Palisades.

Visit us at
www.historypress.com
···